First Ladies Quotation Book

Other books by William O. Foss

Here Is Your Hobby: Skiing
The Norwegian Lady and the Wreck of the Dictator
The United States Navy in Hampton Roads
It Happened First in Virginia
The Lives of Nine Cats

With Erik Bengavst:

Coast Guard in Action
Helicopters in Action
Marine Corps in Action
Skin Divers in Action
Oceanographers in Action

254

255

First Ladies Quotation Book

A Compendium of
Provocative, Tender, Witty and Important Words
From the Presidents' Wives

Compiled and edited
by
William O. Foss

Barricade Books, Inc. New York

Published by Barricade Books Inc.
150 Fifth Avenue
Suite 700
New York, NY 10011

Library of Congress Cataloging-in-Publication Data

Printed in the United States of America.

10 9 8 7 6 5 4 3 2 1

To my sister Beverly Foss Butterworth
and her family.

One of my favorite times was sitting reading quote books, which I did for hours on end . . .

— *Hillary Rodham Clinton*

Contents

Introduction

On my rather untidy bookshelves can be found a number of quotation books, including the classic *Bartlett's Familiar Quotations*, several books devoted to quotations from women of renown, as well as quotation books dealing with love, sports, business, politics, insults and a host of other topics.

Then there's *The World Almanac of Presidential Quotations*, 1993, edited by Elizabeth Frost-Knappmann. Reading this book piqued my curiosity: Was there a book of quotations from all the presidents' wives—the First Ladies? If so, I must add that book to my collection.

After a lengthy search, aided by patient librarians who know how to locate even the most obscure book, I came to the conclusion that the book I wanted had not been written.

Toni Morrison once said, "If there's a book you really want to read but it hasn't been written yet, then you must write it."

So, dear reader, that's how this book came about.

This collection of quotations from the presidents' wives will show their innermost thoughts and feelings about everything from personal affairs to national affairs. Their words vividly reflect their personalities, and should not be taken lightly, for as Canadian poet and novelist Margaret Atwood wrote, "A word after a word after a word is power."

While I intended to limit quotes to the presidential wives who actually served as First Ladies, I am including several statements from Rachel Jackson, who died from a long illness shortly before Andrew Jackson was inaugurated president. The quotations from Rachel Jackson reflect her troubled position on the presidency and the White House.

First Ladies quotations come from statements, letters, speeches, books (some authored by First Ladies), newspapers, magazines, and material obtained from the various presidential libraries and museums.

For readers who may wish to learn more about our First Ladies, I refer you to the bibliography, which lists an array of fine books covering the lives of presidential wives.

W.O.F.

QUOTATIONS

Abandonment

A man can take care of himself. And if he abandons one part of his family he soon learns that he might as well leave them all.

Louisa Adams
Quoted, Jack Shepherd,
Cannibals of the Heart, 1980.

Abortion

The personal thing should be left out of platforms at conventions . . . You can argue yourself blue in the face, and you're not going to change each other's mind. It's a waste of your time and my time.

Barbara Bush
TIME, August 24, 1992.

. . . I feel very strongly that it was the best thing in the world when the Supreme Court voted to legalize abortion, and in my words, bring it out of the backwoods and put it in the hospitals where it belonged. I thought it was a great, great decision.

Betty Ford
60 Minutes, CBS, August 10, 1975.

I'm really not for abortion. I think it's a personal thing.

Patricia Pat Nixon
White House news conference,
August 8, 1972

I'm against abortion on demand except when the mother's life is in danger. I think it's taking a human life, . . .

Nancy Reagan
Quoted, *The New York Times Magazine*, October 26, 1980.

Absence

Your absence begins to be insupportable . . .

> **Louisa Adams**
> Letter to John Quincy Adams,
> June 26, 1804.

It is truly such a state of absence and entire separation as almost amounts to widowhood—and the feeling of dependence on myself alone so different from what I have been accustomed to is excessively painful . . .

> **Jane Pierce**
> Letter to Mary Aiken, June 6, 1847,
> when her husband went away to
> fight in Mexico.

Accomplishment

I feel very comfortable in what I'm doing, and I'm accomplishing something, and that's important.

> **Rosalynn Carter**
> Quoted by Vicki Pearlman,
> "Rosalynn: A Portrait of the First
> Lady," *Atlanta Journal*,
> October 30, 1978.

The satisfaction to do, to accomplish, irrespective of its measure in money or fame, is what should be inculcated. The desire to make the things that are, better,—in a little way with what is at hand,—in a big way if the opportunity comes.

> **Lou Henry Hoover**
> On the upbringing of her two chil-
> dren in the event she or her husband
> should become incapacitated;
> instructions to Jackson E. Reynolds,
> November 24, 1914.

If I stick to this vaguely—I will get lots more accomplished.

Jacqueline Kennedy
Note on her schedule for
October 31, 1962.

What is my proudest accomplishment? I went through some pretty difficult times, and I kept my sanity.

Jacqueline Kennedy Onassis
Quoted in Christopher Andersen,
Jackie After Jack, 1998.

As for accomplishments, I just did what I had to do as things came along.

Eleanor Roosevelt
The New York Times,
October 8, 1954.

You must do the thing you think you cannot do.

Eleanor Roosevelt
You Learn By Living, 1960.

Accountability

If you take on a job, you've got to be accountable for it.

Barbara Bush
Quoted by Henry Louis Gates, Jr.,
The New Yorker, Combined Issue of
February 26 and March 4, 1996.

Achievement

I want him [Jimmy Carter] to succeed, but also, at the same time, I want to be able to do the things that are important to me.

Rosalynn Carter
Quoted, *Newsday's Magazine for
Long Island*, December 3, 1978.

If we have not achieved our early dreams, we must either find new ones or see what we can salvage from the old. If we have accomplished what we set out to do in our youth, then we need not weep like Alexander the Great that we have no more worlds to conquer. There is clearly much left to be done, and whatever else we are going to do, we had better get on with it.

Rosalynn Carter
Everything to Gain, 1987.

There is so much more that I ought to do. My appetite is bigger than my strength—my appetite for information and for contribution.

Claudia Lady Bird Johnson
Ruth Montgomery, *Mrs. LBJ*, 1964.

I always think that it must be a tremendously gratifying thing to feel that you have won out over very great difficulties. If everything was in your favor, if you did not have to surmount any great mountains, then you have nothing to be proud of. But if you feel that you have special difficulties, then you must indeed be proud of your achievement.

Eleanor Roosevelt
Speech, national conference of the National Association for the Advancement of Colored People (NAACP), Richmond, Virginia, July 2, 1939.

Franklin's [D. Roosevelt] death ended a period in history and now in its wake for lots of us who lived his shadow periods have come and we have to start again under our own momentum and wonder what we can achieve.

Eleanor Roosevelt
Letter to Lorena Hickok, April 19, 1945.

Acting

I must say acting was good training for the political life which lay ahead of us.

Nancy Reagan
Nancy, 1980.

Action

I had rather have too much action than too little. Life stagnates without action. I could never bear to merely vegetate.

Abigail Adams
Letter to Elizabeth Shaw Peabody,
June 5, 1809.

If it worries you, then you've got to do something about it.

Barbara Bush
On her feeling that everybody should
help some charitable cause.
The First Ladies, White House
Historical Association, 1994.

I do my own thing. I have things that are important to me, and I do them.

Rosalynn Carter
Quoted, *The New York Times
Magazine*, June 3, 1979.

Once I become involved, I'm in there for a long time.

Nancy Reagan
Interview, *The New York Times*,
February 19, 1982.

I think I have been asked to do something about everything in the world except change the weather!

Eleanor Roosevelt
"Mail of a President's Wife,"
unpublished article, circa 1939.

I have never had to ask permission to do anything in my whole life, I have always done them, and that ended it. And I have seldom even discussed what I was going to do.

Edith Wilson
Letter to Woodrow Wilson,
October 16, 1915

Addiction

I am not only addicted to the medication I have been taking for my arthritis, but also to alcohol.

Betty Ford
Statement issued April 21, 1978,
to reporters at the Long Beach
(California) Naval Hospital, where
she was earlier admitted for
addiction problems.

Admiration

The President [Dwight D. Eisenhower] is a good man and he would always try to do the right thing as he saw it, but he has a great admiration for the achievement of the successful businessman because he has never been a successful businessman and you always admire what you don't really understand.

Eleanor Roosevelt
Interview, Meet the Press, NBC-TV,
September 16, 1956.

Advice

Show me a wife who doesn't offer advice, and I'll show you one who doesn't care very much.

Barbara Bush
Houston Post, January 15, 1989.

I tell him [Jimmy Carter] what I think.

Rosalynn Carter
Interview, *The New York Times*,
March 10, 1977.

People have written that I'm Jimmy's greatest adviser, and so forth. I'm not. But I talk to him about all the things he's trying to do. If there's something that involves the elderly, women's issues, the mentally ill, things that I know about, that I feel I can advise him on, I do it. And he trusts my opinion because he knows that I've worked on these things for a long time. I don't even try to advise him on a lot of things. But I can talk to him about what I feel ought to be done. He talks to me about welfare, tax reform, and I tell what I think about it. I don't say, do this or do that, I've never done that. And I'm not saying that he always does what I want him to do. But he always listens.

Rosalynn Carter
The New Republic, August 19, 1978.

Don't mope around the house. Attend operas and concerts.

Mary Lincoln
Advice to her daughter-in-law
Mary Harlan Lincoln, fall of 1889.

. . . I hasten to give you freely that which you ask me, "the advice of a mother,"—It is, that you immediately secure for your life & even after, the lonely one who has promised you her hand—she who I am persuaded would be a prize to any man—Why then should delay obstruct your happiness, . . .

Dolley Madison
Letter to her nephew, Edward D. Cutts,
October 30, 1844.

I don't claim to advise him [Richard M. Nixon]. He's a pretty strong man.

Patricia Pat Nixon
Quoted, *The New York Times*,
January 26, 1970.

Affection

You know, my friend, I am not ambitious of anything but your affection and in that my wishes are unbounded.

Luisa Adams
Letter to John Quincy Adams,
July 4, 1796.

Affirmative Action

Affirmative action has helped on the one hand because it has given opportunities to many people to prove themselves, which they have done. But I think that it has hurt because I believe it has been misconstrued and misunderstood and used as a negative.

Hillary Rodham Clinton
Comments at an event sponsored by
the Team Harmony Foundation to
help school children combat bigotry;
Boston, Massachusetts,
December 9, 1997.

Afterlife

The change from this gloomy earth, to be forever reunited with my idolized husband & my darling Willie, would be happiness indeed!

Mary Lincoln
Letter to Mrs. Slataper,
September 29, 1868.

Aging

I'm old enough . . . I'm really half a century old! Think about that. . . . It's hard to believe it happens!

Hillary Rodham Clinton
Comments, University of Maryland,
College Park, Maryland,
October 3, 1997.

Turning fifty doesn't bother me. Being told or sort of realizing that I'm half a century old, that's different.

Hillary Rodham Clinton
News conference,
October 10, 1997.

Yes, Dr. Peschau, I'm growing old, I grow old willingly; I grow old not unwillingly.

Sarah Childress Polk
Comments to the Reverend Peschau,
once a pastor of the German
Lutheran Church in Nashville,
Tennessee. Anson and Fanny Nelson,
Memorials of Sarah Childress Polk,
1892.

Of course I haven't changed a bit, except to improve, etc. etc.

Julia Gardiner Tyler
Letter to her mother, Juliana Gardiner,
February 4, 1861.

Agreement

I don't agree with George Bush on every issue, and I don't expect him to agree with me on every issue, . . . but we are in agreement on most of the important things.

Barbara Bush
Interview, *The New York Times*,
February 22, 1981.

Alcoholism

Since the disease affects the entire family, counseling should be available to all family members.

Betty Ford
Discussing alcoholism treatment
before a meeting of the National
Association of Insurance
Commissioners, New York,
December 2, 1980.

Alzheimer's Disease

No one is immune. Families really need help to understand it and cope with it.

> **Nancy Reagan**
> *Newsweek*, October 2, 1995.

Ambition

O Ambition how many actions dost thou make poor mortals commit!

> **Abigail Adams**
> Letter to Mercy Otis Warren,
> November 5, 1775.

Ah! but I am ambitious! And the best of it is that mine is gratified ambition, for I am ambitious for you—and for myself, too . . .

> **Ellen Axson Wilson**
> Letter to Woodrow Wilson,
> April 11, 1885.

America/American

Don't you think this little Spot of ours better calculated for happiness than any other you have yet seen or read of?

> **Abigail Adams**
> Letter to Isaac Smith, Jr.,
> April 20, 1771.

. . . whatever my fair countrywomen may think, and I hear they envy my situation, I will most joyfully exchange Europe for America, and my public for a private life. I am really surfeited with Europe, and most heartily long for the rural cottage, the purer and honester manners of my native land, where domestic happiness reigns unrivalled, and virtue and honor go hand in hand.

> **Abigail Adams**
> Letter to Thomas Jefferson,
> February 11, 1786.

The people of this country are not weak, not cowardly and not spiritually exhausted. There is a pervasive desire among Americans to live a useful life, to correct the defects in our society, and to make our nation even greater than it already is.

> **Rosalynn Carter**
> Speech, National Press Club,
> Washington, D.C., June 20, 1978.

I am so proud to be an American.

> **Mamie Eisenhower**
> Comments during Flag Day
> observances in the U.S. House of
> Representatives, June 14, 1971.

. . . we have a can-do country.

> **Claudia Lady Bird Johnson**
> Speech at luncheon by the Federated
> Democratic Women of Ohio,
> Columbus, Ohio, September 18, 1964.

The American eagle flaps its wings when I think of all I have seen since leaving home. Country and countrymen I am proud of them both. . . . This is a great, big overgrown, hobbledehoy of a nation, and may it be long before its angles wear off.

> **Edith Kermit Roosevelt**
> Letter to Cecil Spring-Rice,
> April 5, 1911; commenting on her
> trip to Yosemite.

. . . I think our country afford everything that can give pleasure or satisfaction to a rational mind . . .

> **Martha Washington**
> Letter to Janet Livingston
> Montgomery, January 29, 1791.

Army Women

I have always found Army women particularly delightful, and it is easy to understand why they are so. In course of their wanderings and their many changes of habitation, and in consequence of the happy-go-lucky attitude toward life that they are bound to assume, they acquire a cordiality of manner and an all-round generous tone which make them very attractive.

Helen Taft
Recollections of Full Years, 1914.

Arts

All of our artists and cultural institutions are an integral part of what we call America, and . . . we must work very hard not only to preserve and nurture, but to love [them] because of the impact they make on our lives.

Hillary Rodham Clinton
Comments before a public meeting of the President's Committee on the Arts and Humanities, Washington, D.C., December 2, 1994.

Art is a vital part of our national character. Art in all its forms unites our people, for it speaks the common language of our intellect, our emotion and our spirit.

Hillary Rodham Clinton
Speech at the presentation of National Heritage Fellowships by the National Endowment for the Arts, White House, September 27, 1995.

As we prepare for a new century, and yes, a new millennium, the arts and humanities are more essential than ever to the endurance of our democratic values of tolerance, pluralism and freedom at a time when so much else is happening to change the way we work and live.

Hillary Rodham Clinton
Commenting on a report promoting
America's arts and humanities;
Washington, D.C.,
February 29, 1997.

. . . art is the window to man's soul. Without it, he would never be able to see beyond his immediate world; nor could the world see the man within.

Claudia Lady Bird Johnson
Speech, Museum of Modern Art,
New York, May 25, 1964.

If we gain nothing but acceptance of the fact that Government has an interest in the development of artistic expression—no matter how that expression comes, and if we have been able to widen the interest of the people as a whole in art, we have reaped a really golden harvest out of what many of us feel have been barren years.

Eleanor Roosevelt
Speech, 25th annual convention of
the American Federation of Artists,
May 16, 1934.

An artist—if he doesn't create what he really sees and feels—is not an artist.

Eleanor Roosevelt
Discussing art appreciation, Chicago
Round Table broadcast, *NBC*,
November 24, 1940.

. . . my talent for art combined with my talent for work might, after many years, win me a place in the first rank among American artists.

Ellen Axson Wilson
Letter to Woodrow Wilson, March
28, 1885, when she was studying at
the Arts Students League in New York.

Assassination

I tried to express something of how we felt. I said, "Oh, Mrs. Kennedy, you know we never even wanted to be Vice President and now, Dear God, it's come to this." I would have done anything to help her, but there was nothing I could do to help her . . .

Claudia Lady Bird Johnson
Describing her attempt to comfort Jacqueline Kennedy after the assassination of President Kennedy. Taped statement to the President's Commission on the Assassination of John F. Kennedy, submitted July 16, 1964.

My Dearest was receiving in a public hall on our return, when he was shot . . .

Ida McKinley
Diary, September 6, 1901. President McKinley was mortally wounded by an assassin on September 6, 1901, when he and his wife attended the Pan-American Exposition in Buffalo, New York. He died September 14, 1901.

. . . I just remember falling on him and saying, "Oh, no, no," I mean, "Oh, my God, they have shot my husband." And "I love you, Jack," I remember I was shouting. And just being down in the car with his head in my lap. And it just seemed eternity.

Jacqueline Kennedy
Describing the assassination of President John F. Kennedy in Dallas, November 22, 1963. Testimony before the President's Commission on the Assassination of John F. Kennedy, New York, June 5, 1964.

I want them to see what they have done to Jack.

Jacqueline Kennedy
To Lady Bird Johnson, declining the
offer to help change her blood-
stained clothes after her husband
was assassinated in Dallas, Texas,
November 22, 1963.
From the White House diary tapes of
Mrs. Claudia Lady Bird Johnson,
covering the period
November 22–24, 1963.

When will our country learn that to live by the sword is to perish by
the sword? I pray that with the price he paid—his life—he will make
room in people's hearts for love, not hate.

Jacqueline Kennedy
Statement issued April 5, 1968,
New York, on the assassination of Dr.
Martin Luther King Jr.

Assistance

Another thing most of us were taught early in school that we
shouldn't forget when you get older is: Help your classmates . . . help
your fellow human beings.

Barbara Bush
Commencement address, Bennett
College, Greensboro, North Carolina,
May 14, 1989.

I think I am the person closest to the President of the United States,
and if I can help him understand the countries of the world, then
that's what I intend to do.

Rosalynn Carter
Response when asked by a reporter
during an overseas trip what it was
that made her think that she was fit
to discuss serious matters with heads
of state. *Time,* June 13, 1977.

Athletics

I myself am very athletic but I have never been able to throw a ball as far as a man.

Barbara Bush
Press conference, White House,
January 16, 1990.

Atomic Bomb

I think if the atomic bomb did nothing more, it scared the people to the point where they realize that either they must do something about preventing war or there is a chance that there might be a morning when we would not wake up.

Eleanor Roosevelt
Press conference, January 3, 1946.

It is always hard to tell people that it is the causes of war which bring about such things as Hiroshima, and that we must try to eliminate these causes because if there is another Pearl Harbor there will be undoubtedly another Hiroshima.

Eleanor Roosevelt
Letter to John Golden,
June 12, 1953.

Attractiveness

You may not believe it, but I never used to think much about my looks if I knew my dress was all right; now I do care about being pretty for you, and every girl I see I think "I wonder if I am as pretty as she," or "At any rate I am not quite as ugly as that girl."

Edith Kermit Roosevelt
Letter to Theodore Roosevelt,
June 8, 1886.

. . . no matter how plain a woman may be if truth & loyalty are stamped on her face all will be attracted to her . . .

Eleanor Roosevelt
Writings at the age of fourteen.

Auctions

My slogan is "Never come home empty-handed."

Grace Coolidge
On her passion for auctions in a round robin letter to her friends, 1937.

Authenticity

I wouldn't put on a mask and pretend to be anything that I wasn't.

Jacqueline Kennedy
Interview, *The New York Times*,
September 20, 1960.

Avocations

I have a great many avocations of one kind or another which imperceptibly consume my time.

Martha Washington
Letter to Mercy Warren,
June 12, 1790.

Baseball

I venture to say that not one of you care one hoot about baseball but to me it is my very life.

Grace Coolidge
Round robin letter to her friends,
July 8, 1955.

Battles

I like to fight my own battles.

Patricia Pat Nixon
Comment to a White House staffer.

Beauty/Beautification

. . . the things worth remembering in a lifetime are often—with me—associated with beauty.

Claudia Lady Bird Johnson
U.S. News & World Report,
February 22, 1965.

Beauty is a fragile word. Once its use was reserved for the tender little lady who did needlepoint. Politically, it has been an almost embarrassing word. Few men of business or politics would talk of "beauty."

Claudia Lady Bird Johnson
Speech, annual convention of the
Associated Press Managing Editors
Association, Washington, D.C.,
October 1, 1965.

Beautification is not only for people, it is by people too . . .

Claudia Lady Bird Johnson
Letter to Polly Shackleton,
January 26, 1966.

. . . beautification means our total concern for the physical and human quality of the world we pass on to our children.

Claudia Lady Bird Johnson
Address at Yale Political Union,
New Haven, Connecticut,
October 9, 1967.

My mother was always a little troubled by my lack of beauty, and I knew it as a child senses those things. She tried very hard to bring me up well so my manners would in some way compensate for my looks, but her efforts only made me more keenly conscious of my shortcomings.

> **Eleanor Roosevelt**
> *This Is My Story*, 1937.

Bed/Bedtime

. . . every woman over fifty should stay in bed until noon.

> **Mamie Eisenhower**
> Quoted, Stephen Ambrose,
> *Eisenhower*, 1983.

It is rare for either of us to go to bed much before 12 or 1 o'clock.

> **Eleanor Roosevelt**
> On life in the White House,
> radio broadcast, *NBC*,
> September 25, 1934.

The General always retires at nine, and I usually precede him.

> **Martha Washington**
> Quoted, Anne Hollingsworth
> Wharton, *Martha Washington*, 1897.

Behavior

I very well know every eye is upon me, my dear mother, and I will behave accordingly.

> **Julia Tyler**
> Letter to her mother, Juliana
> Gardiner, July 1844. Mrs. Gardiner
> had advised her daughter to observe
> proper decorum as the young
> mistress of the White House.

Bookkeeping

This was an undertaking for me, for, to tell the truth, my little book never, no never, added quite right.

> **Julia Dent Grant**
> On keeping an account book. *The Personal Memoirs of Julia Dent Grant,* 1975.

Books

[John Quincy Adams] reads a page in every book that passes through his hands.

> **Louisa Adams**
> Complaining that her husband's book reading slowed the work of moving into a rented house. From her diary, "The Adventures of a Nobody."

One of my favorite times was sitting reading quote books, which I did for hours on end . . . [while writing her own book, *It Takes a Village: And Other Lessons Children Teach Us*].

> **Hillary Rodham Clinton**
> Interview, *C-SPAN Booknotes,* March 3, 1996.

People are my books.

> **Grace Coolidge**
> Response when asked about her favorite reading. Quoted, Bess Furman, *White House Profile,* 1951.

. . . I enjoy, as always, spending some time reading the Bible. To me it's the most fascinating book in the world.

> **Betty Ford**
> Interview, *U.S. News & World Report,* October 18, 1976.

I like to read most when I'm stretched out in bed, ready to relax and ultimately drop off to sleep. Another time is on a trip, when I like to put two or three books in a straw bag to have handy.

Claudia Lady Bird Johnson
The New York Times Book Review,
July 4, 1965.

I love to stay home two or three nights a week and read [books].

Claudia Lady Bird Johnson
Interview, *The New York Times*,
March 22, 1982.

By the bye, do you ever get hold of a clever novel, new or old, that you could send me? I bought [James Fenimore] Cooper's last, but did not care for it, because the story was so full of horrors.

Dolley Madison
Letter to her niece, Dolley Cutts,
March 10, 1830.

Before we were married, whenever he [John F. Kennedy] gave me a present it was usually a book. History. Biography.

Jacqueline Kennedy
Interview by Henry Fonda, CBS-TV,
November 2, 1960.

I have many books presented to me by writers, and I try to read them all; at present that is impossible, but this evening the author of this book dines with the President, and I could not be so unkind as to appear wholly ignorant and unmindful of his gift.

Sarah Childress Polk
Quoted by Mrs. Maury, an
Englishwoman; cited in Anson and
Fanny Nelson, *Memorials of Sarah
Childress Polk*, 1892.

. . . while one can lose oneself in a book one can never be thoroughly unhappy.

Edith Roosevelt
Letter to Theodore Roosevelt,
June 8, 1886.

The books that we give our children to read are strong influences in the shaping of their future lives. In them they find the material for their adult standards, ideals and taste.

Eleanor Roosevelt
Statement at Authors Dinner,
New York, January 25, 1933.

He [Woodrow Wilson] was one of the best readers I have ever heard, and he loved books and good English so that his own keen appreciation and enthusiasm added beauty to them.

Edith Wilson
My Memoir, 1939.

And of course there were books and books.

Edith Wilson, describing the books
President Wilson brought from the White House to his new home in Washington, D.C. *My Memoir*, 1939.

George Bush

There is no more honest man.

Barbara Bush
Interview, *The Washington Post*,
August 21, 1984.

I really think he has to run again, honestly. . . . Now, I don't want that to be a public announcement.

Barbara Bush
Interview in Moscow, ABC,
July 11, 1991.

Campaigning

I was really surprised to discover that I enjoyed campaigning. It was like being sent on a vacation.

Barbara Bush
Interview, *The New York Times*,
February 22, 1981.

Everybody is so enthusiastic in the country. . . . We're too sophisticated in Washington.

Barbara Bush
Comments while campaigning in
Los Angeles, June 1988.

The trouble with me is I adore campaigns.

Barbara Bush
Press conference, White House,
January 16, 1990.

Ugly things don't win campaigns. . . . I think you win if you stay above board and stick to the facts.

Barbara Bush
Former First Ladies Forum, Kennedy
Center, Washington, D.C.,
March 9, 1998.

It's a labor of love.

Rosalynn Carter
Kandy Stroud, *How Jimmy Won*,
1977.

I just love campaigning, love meeting new people, and talking to them.

Rosalynn Carter
Comments made on the 1980 presidential campaign trail.

It was not a vocation I would want to pursue for life.

Rosalynn Carter
First Lady from Plains, 1984.

If you vote for him, you get me.

Hillary Rodham Clinton
The Washington Post, March 10, 1992.

I know you think I'm nuts but I find this exciting.

Hillary Rodham Clinton
Remark to a reporter of her love of campaigning during the 1992 presidential election campaign.

I'm going to continue to do what I've done for more than twenty years of marriage, which is support my husband.

Hillary Rodham Clinton
Reply to reporter when asked what her role would be in the 1996 presidential election campaign.

I have spoken, I've gone door-to-door, I like grass roots, precinct, door-to-door.

Betty Ford
Telling reporters how she had campaigned for her husband in Congressional races; press conference, Los Angeles, May 18, 1975.

. . . I don't want you to come back here and talk Warren into running for President, for I do not intend to permit him to run. Because of the condition of his health it would bring a tragedy to us both.

Florence Harding
To E. Mont Reily, who was among those who tried to push her husband into the Republican presidential nomination in 1920.

Give up? Not until the convention is over. Think of your friends in Ohio.

Florence Harding
To Warren Harding, who was ready to withdraw from the presidential race after finishing third in the Indiana primary, May 1920.

Our escort consisted of the Chief of Police in his car and twenty-four of Cleveland's "finest" mounted police on splendid Ky. horses—ten plain clothes secret-service men and Heaven knows what else. . . . well I was quite thrilled and enjoyed the "Show."

Florence Harding
Undated [1920] letter to
Frank C. Scobey, a personal friend of
her husband.

So glad all y'all came.

Claudia Lady Bird Johnson
Campaign greeting.

Campaigning . . . is the greatest adventure anyone can have.

Claudia Lady Bird Johnson
The New York Times,
December 15, 1963.

I do [find campaigning tiring], but at the same time it's exhilarating meeting people I remember, so I don't get too tired.

Jacqueline Kennedy
Comments while campaigning with
her husband in Wheeling, West
Virginia; interview, *WTRF-TV,*
April 19, 1960.

My husband and I always campaign together as a team. I go around with him and talk to the women.

Patricia Pat Nixon
The Washington Post, July 14, 1952.

I haven't had so much fun in a long time.

Patricia Pat Nixon
To news reporters aboard a jet plane
during the campaign,
September 23, 1972.

It is only the hope that you can live through [the campaign] that gives me a prospect of enjoyment.

Sarah Childress Polk
Letter to James Polk,
March 29, 1843.

Always be on time. Do as little talking as humanly possible. Remember to lean back in the parade car so everybody can see the President. Be sure not to get too fat, because you'll have to sit there in the back seat.

Eleanor Roosevelt
On campaign behavior for first
ladies. *The New York Times*,
November 11, 1962.

Camping

I adore camping—camping alone with my family and a few friends far off in the mountains . . .

Lou Henry Hoover
Radio broadcast, NBC, to 4-H Boys
and Girls Clubs, June 22, 1929.

Candidness

My husband always enjoined upon me to be quiet . . .

Mary Lincoln
Letter to Alexander Williamson,
December 14, 1866.

Career

Ike was my career.

Mamie Eisenhower
Julie Nixon Eisenhower, *Special
People*, 1977.

I have but one career and its name is Ike.

Mamie Eisenhower
J. B. West, *Upstairs at the White House*, 1973.

If the career is the husband's, the wife can merge her own with it, if it is to be the wife's as it undoubtedly will be in an increasing proportion of cases, then the husband may, with no sacrifice of self respect or of recognition by the community, permit himself to be the less prominent and distinguished member of the combination.

Florence Harding
Letter, February 7, 1922.

It is perfectly possible to have both a home and a career, [for] in this modern age we are released from so many of the burdens our grandmothers and great-grandmothers had to bear.

Lou Henry Hoover
Comments at a regional Girl Scout conference, Duluth, Minnesota, May 26, 1936.

A man has a right to make his own decision about his career and a woman should support that decision.

Patricia Pat Nixon
Good Housekeeping, July 1971.

I think if you really put your whole heart into something and work for it, you generally end up liking it.

Patricia Pat Nixon
Helen Thomas, *Dateline: White House*, 1975.

A career myself? Never! I have the only one I want . . .

Bess Truman
Chicago Daily News, April 13, 1945.

Caregivers

All caregivers [of the terminally ill] feel guilty, even if they are available twenty-four hours a day. I feel very guilty about my mother; she's ninety-one, and she wants me to be in Plains, Georgia, all the time. She doesn't like it when I travel. But if caregivers don't watch out for themselves, they'll lose the ability to truly help their loved ones. The best thing a person who is devoted to a dying family member can do is to be involved in a support group.

> **Rosalynn Carter**
> Interview, *U.S. News & World Report*, February 24, 1997.

Caring

Why is it that in a country as economically wealthy as we are, in a country with the longest surviving democracy, there is this undercurrent of discontent? That we lack at some core level meaning in our individual lives and meaning collectively. . . . We need a new ethos of individual responsibility and caring. . . . we have to summon up what we believe is morally and ethically and spiritually correct and do the best that we can with God's guidance.

> **Hillary Rodham Clinton**
> Speech, University of Texas, Austin, Texas, April 6, 1993.

Carpenter

. . . in the process I have become a very respectable carpenter.

> **Rosalynn Carter**
> On volunteering with her husband to help build homes for Habitat for Humanity.
> Address at the Riverside Baptist Church, Washington, D.C., May 5, 1989.

Jimmy Carter

Jimmy talks too much, but at least he's honest . . .

Rosalynn Carter
Comments upon public reaction to
Jimmy Carter's interview with
Playboy in which he confessed to
"lusting in my heart" for other
women; *First Lady from Plains*, 1984.

Jimmy will be remembered for peace and human rights and his
compassion and caring for other people.

Rosalynn Carter
Interview, *The Washington Post*,
April 25, 1984.

He tends to appear naive . . . I don't like it . . . but it's important to
him to be that way.

Rosalynn Carter
On her husband as a negotiator, *Life*,
November 1995.

Challenges

The challenges facing us today are not the same as those that faced
our parents and our grandparents. There are common threads which
run through them, that demand the best from us. And the answers,
I believe, are rooted in the same values and attitudes that really
created the climate of change that America has always been able to
respond to.

Hillary Rodham Clinton
Speech, Joint Armed Forces Wives'
Luncheon, November 19, 1993.

Change

Eleanor Roosevelt

All change probably arose in the first place because of women. If you think back a little bit and think of the old cave-dwelling days, I think you will agree with me that the first step probably to a little more comfort and a little better food came because the woman was not quite satisfied with the original cave. . . . So the original cave man was pushed to make some change, and gradually as we follow down through history, I think we will find that much of the effort of man is due to the desire for change in women.

Eleanor Roosevelt
Speech, Chautauqua Women's Club,
Chautauqua, New York,
July 25, 1933.

We started from scratch, every American an immigrant who came because he wanted change.

Eleanor Roosevelt
Tomorrow Is Now, 1963.

I do not like people who change their minds so quickly . . .

Edith Wilson
My Memoir, 1939.

Character

The Natural tenderness and Delicacy of our Constitution, added to the many Dangers we are subject to from your Sex, renders it almost impossible for a Single Lady to travel without injury to her Character.

Abigail Adams
Letter to Isaac Smith, Jr.,
April 20, 1771.

There are times in which a Genius would wish to live. It is not in the still calm of life, or the repose of a pacific station, that great characters are formed. Great necessities call out great virtues. When a mind is raised and animated by scenes that engage the heart, then those qualities, which would wise lie dormant wake into life and form the character of the Hero and the Statesman.

Abigail Adams
Letter to John Quincy Adams,
January 19, 1780.

A good coat is tantamount to a good character and if the world be a stage it's necessary to dress as to act your part as well.

Abigail Adams
Letter to John Quincy Adams,
December 18, 1804.

We believe that the character of a people depends mainly on its homes.

Lucy Hayes
Address as president of the Women's
Home Missionary Society, 1894.

I place my faith in the individual development of character. Human nature changes very little. If girls and boys grow up in an atmosphere of frankness and fair play and consideration for others, and with a sense of responsibility toward their own families and communities, then they are as safe today as they were when I was young.

Eleanor Roosevelt
Radio broadcast, *NBC*,
December 23, 1932.

I have always felt that anyone who wanted an election so much that they would use those methods [referring to Richard Nixon's smear campaign against Helen Gahagan Douglas] did not have the character that I really admired in public life.

Eleanor Roosevelt
Meet the Press, NBC-TV,
September 16, 1956.

Charity

It is part of religion as well as morality to do justly and to love mercy and a man cannot be an honest and zealous promoter of the principles of a true government without possessing that good will towards man which leads to the love of God and respect for the Deity.

Agibail Adams
Letter to Mary Cranch,
May 26, 1798.

Since leaving the White House, Jimmy and I have had few experiences more personally fulfilling than building homes with Habitat.

Rosalynn Carter
Letter supporting volunteer
program of Habitat for Humanity
International, 1998.

Cheerfulness

Life is sort of sad, so I tried to cheer everybody up. I learned to be that kind of person.

Patricia Pat Nixon
Quoted, Julie Nixon Eisenhower,
Pat Nixon: The Untold Story, 1978.

Cheerleader

I'm a giant cheerleader. I'm cheering for teachers who are underpaid, under praised and overworked.

Barbara Bush
Address during a luncheon sponsored
by Links Inc., Washington, D.C.,
March 21, 1982.

Chicago

Chicago is my kind of village.

Hillary Rodham Clinton
Speech, Democratic National
Convention, Chicago,
August 27, 1996.

. . . beautiful city of Chicago with its parks . . . and the great Lake spreading far beyond our sight.

Lucy Hayes
Letter to her son Scott Hayes,
September 9, 1878

There is no more expensive place than Chicago.

Mary Lincoln
Letter to Alexander Williamson,
November 10, 1867.

Children

I have always thought it of very great importance that children should, in the early part of life, be unaccustomed to such examples as would tend to corrupt the purity of their words and actions that they may chill with horror at the sound of an oath and blush with indignation at an obscene expression. These first principals which grow with their growth and strengthen with their strength neither time or custom can totally eradicate.

Abigail Adams
Letter to John Adams,
September 16, 1774.

. . . not teach them what to think, but how to think, and they will learn how to act.

Abigail Adams
Paul G. Nagel, *Descent from Glory: Four Generations of the John Adams Family*, 1983.

My children seem to have some intemperate blood in them and are certainly not very easy to govern.

Louisa Adams
Diary, November 15, 1820.

I don't think men and women should have children and not take responsibility.

Barbara Bush
Interview, *The New York Times*,
April 8, 1984.

You got to put your children first. If you opt to have children, no matter what your occupation, you got to take care of them.

Barbara Bush
Former First Ladies Forum, Kennedy
Center, Washington, D.C.,
March 9, 1998.

I've been proud of the way my children reacted to the pressures [of living in the White House].

Rosalynn Carter
Interview, *The Washington Post*,
November 19, 1980.

I will be the voice for children.

Hillary Rodham Clinton
Commenting on her role as First
Lady; news conference, New York,
July 11, 1992.

I'm often asked what I would like to see happen above all else in our country and in the world. There are so many things to pray for, so many things to work for. But certainly my answer would be a world in which all boys and girls are loved and cared for. First, by the families into which they are born, and then by all of us who have to recognize that we are all connected. Nothing is more important to our shared future than the well-being of children.

Hillary Rodham Clinton
Body Mind Spirit, October-
November 1995.

There is no such thing as other people's children.

Hillary Rodham Clinton
Newsweek, January 15, 1996.

No country does enough to invest in its children or families.

Hillary Rodham Clinton
Comments made in Athens, Greece,
March 29, 1996.

We are all responsible for assuring that children are raised in a nation that doesn't just talk about family values, but acts in ways that values families.

Hillary Rodham Clinton
Speech, Democratic National
Convention, Chicago,
August 27, 1996.

How we care for our children is critical to their intellectual and emotional development.

Hillary Rodham Clinton
Speech, University of Maryland,
College Park, Maryland,
October 3, 1997.

Too often parents are better informed on what car to buy than what kind of child care to choose.

Hillary Rodham Clinton
Speech, University of Maryland,
College Park, Maryland,
October 3, 1997.

. . . if you don't invest [time and activity] in your children, at the end of the day, you know, you haven't really done the most important job you have been given to do.

Hillary Rodham Clinton
Comments on Oprah Winfrey show,
Oprah, ABC-TV,
October 28, 1997.

I feel that God gives us these children and expects us to do the best we can with them for a certain time. Then they are on their own.

Betty Ford
McCall's, February 1975.

I believe that children are given to you for a certain period of time and I think if you can't shape their lives by the time they are 18 and leaving for college or going out in the world, it's pretty hard to do much more after that.

Betty Ford
Interview, *The New York Times*,
January 14, 1977.

There is nothing more discouraging than a moody, complaining child . . .

Lou Henry Hoover
Radio address to 4-H Clubs, *NBC*,
March 7, 1931.

My own recipe for raising them [daughters Lynda and Lucy] is to give them a considerable sense of independence, and yet let them know that I trust them a lot and am there to see what comes through.

Claudia Lady Bird Johnson
Ruth Montgomery, *Mrs. LBJ*, 1964.

People have too many theories about rearing children. I believe simply in love, security, and discipline.

Jacqueline Kennedy
Statement, 1959.

. . . I don't want my children brought up by nurses and Secret Service men.

Jacqueline Kennedy
Press conference, Hyannis Port,
Massachusetts, November 10, 1960.

Most important, of course, is not to shut off the inquiring mind by being impatient with its questions. The seemingly endless chain of "whys" means something important to the child—his way of learning.

Jacqueline Kennedy
Ontario Windsor Star,
November 15, 1960.

No fathers or mothers can be happy until they have the possibility of jobs and education for their children. This must be for all and not just a few.

Jacqueline Kennedy
Speech in Venezuela,
December 1961.

It isn't fair to children in the limelight to leave them to the care of others and then to expect that they will turn out all right. They need their mother's affection and guidance and long period of time alone with her. That is what gives them security in an often confusing new world.

Jacqueline Kennedy
Interview, *The Associated Press*,
July 21, 1962.

. . . if you bungle raising your children, I don't think whatever else you do well matters very much.

Jacqueline Kennedy
Theodore C. Sorenson,
Kennedy, 1965.

[she found it] . . . a relief to know that other people's children are as bad . . . at the same age.

Jacqueline Kennedy
On the mischief and misbehavior of her children in the White House.
Theodore C. Sorensen,
Kennedy, 1965.

The greatest responsibility is your children. If my children turned out badly, I'd feel that nothing I had done was worthwhile.

Jacqueline Kennedy
Quoted by Ruth Montgomery,
Hail to the Chiefs, 1970.

. . . do not allow the baby to walk too soon or she will become bowlegged.

Mary Lincoln
Advice to her daughter-in-law Mary
Harlan Lincoln on the raising of her
granddaughter Mary, fall of 1869.

The 60's were a difficult time to bring up a child and to be a child. Certainly they were exposed to things that we were never exposed to.

Nancy Reagan
Quoted, *The New York Times*
Magazine, October 26, 1980.

Children are such queer little people and all their imaginings are so matter of fact, drawn from their own experience which necessarily is very limited, and from whatever they hear or read which impresses them very deeply.

Edith Kermit Roosevelt
Letter to Theodore Roosevelt,
June 8, 1886.

. . . there is no other child in the world that is so greatly pampered as the American child.

Eleanor Roosevelt
Interview, *The New York Times*,
April 20, 1924.

I was brought up to observe strict obedience to my parents and not to ask questions. You cannot do that with children today, and we cannot bring them up as we were raised.

Eleanor Roosevelt
Address, Institute for Advanced
Education, New York,
March 8, 1932.

You seem to think that everyone can save money if they have the character to do it. As a matter of fact, there are innumerable people who have a wide choice between saving and giving their children the best possible opportunities. The decision is usually in favor of the children.

> **Eleanor Roosevelt**
> Letter to Franklin D. Roosevelt III,
> January 15, 1962.

I used to say she was a very good baby as babies go, but now I declare her a perfect cherub.

> **Ellen Axson Wilson**
> Praising her first child, daughter
> Margaret Axson Wilson, in a letter to
> Woodrow Wilson, June 6, 1886.

Children and Parents

I think children have a tendency to take parents for granted, and it isn't until they are confronted with a danger of serious illness or the possibility of losing them that they learn how much they really care.

> **Betty Ford**
> *McCall's*, February 1975.

I want my children to know that their concerns—their doubts and their difficulties—whatever they may be, can be discussed with the two people in this world who care the most—their mother and father.

> **Betty Ford**
> Letter written in September 1975 to
> Lorena Chevalier of Dallas, who had
> written to Mrs. Ford about her
> appearance on a "60 Minutes"
> television interview. Mrs. Ford was
> criticized for saying she "wouldn't
> be surprised" if her 18-year
> daughter, Susan, told her she was
> having an affair.

Choice

Decisions are not irrevocable. Choices do come back.

Barbara Bush
Commencement address, Wellesley
College, Wellesley, Massachusetts,
June 1, 1990.

I suppose I could have stayed home, baked cookies and had teas, but what I decided to do is to fulfill my profession, which I entered before my husband was in public office. . . . The work that I've done as a professional, as a public advocate, has been aimed in part to assure that women can make the choices that they should make—whether it's full-time career, full-time motherhood, some combination, depending upon what stage of life they are at—and I think that is still difficult for people to understand right now, that it is a generational change.

Hillary Rodham Clinton
Comments to reporters on campaign
trail, Chicago, March 16, 1992.

What is marvelous and wonderful about coming of age in America today, despite all of the problems that we face, is you do have so many more choices to craft your own life than any generation had.

Hillary Rodham Clinton
Commencement address, George
Washington University,
Washington, D.C., May 8, 1994.

Christian/Christianity

I have dipped into others [philosophers] and thrown them aside, but I have never seen anything that would satisfy my mind, or that would compare with the chaste and exquisitely simple doctrines of Christianity.

Louisa Adams
Letter to her father-in-law,
John Adams, April 16, 1819.

I have to confess [expressing it jokingly] that it's crossed my mind that you could not be a Republican and a Christian from time to time. [After noting how hurt she had been by conservatives who proclaim that it is impossible to be both a Democrat and a Christian.]

Hillary Rodham Clinton
Speech at the Nation Prayer
Breakfast, Washington Hilton,
Washington, D.C., February 6, 1997.

Christmas

Christmas is a time when we're supposed to not only think about our blessings but also about what it means to be a peacemaker. And certainly, this past year, the United States and the president have shown what it takes to make peace in lots of places in the world. It is not easy. It's not sure. But we're not guaranteed that. But what we have to do is to keep trying.

Hillary Rodham Clinton
Interview, *Larry King Live*, CNN,
December 23, 1995.

It takes a lot of work to get ready for Christmas in the White House.

Hillary Rodham Clinton
Comments, "Christmas in
Washington," *NBC-TV*,
December 19, 1997.

As you grow older you are more aware of the true meaning of Christmas and how it brings out the nicest, kindest, gentlest qualities in people, qualities you wish would continue all year long.

Nancy Reagan
"Christmas Memories" by Nancy
Reagan, *The Washington Post*,
December 16, 1982.

Citizens

I'm not exactly your average citizen.

Barbara Bush
Press conference, White House,
March 29, 1989.

Good home makers . . . are good citizens.

Lou Henry Hoover
Speech, 25th National Girl Scout
Convention, Philadelphia, 1939.

Civic Life

Women can do much in their civic life. They can alert citizens to be interested in the affairs of their city. They can push and prod legislature. They can raise sights and set standards . . . For me, and probably for most women, the attempt to become an involved citizen has been a matter of evolution rather than choice . . .

Claudia Lady Bird Johnson
Statement issued from the
White House, August 22, 1964.

Civilian Life

The world outside [the Army] is pretty cold and impersonal.

Mamie Eisenhower
Letter to Mrs. Alfred M. Gruenther,
April 24, 1956.

Civil Rights

We are a nation of laws, not men, and our greatness is our ability to adjust to the national consensus.

Claudia Lady Bird Johnson
Elizabeth Carpenter,
Ruffles & Flourishes, 1993.

I believe that you must apply to all groups the right to all forms of thoughts, to all forms of expression.

Eleanor Roosevelt
Address to the Chicago Civil Liberties
Committee, March 14, 1940.

Civil War

How many homes made desolate! How many hearts broken! How much youth sacrificed!

Julia Dent Grant
After seeing fallen Richmond,
Virginia. *The Personal Memoirs of
Julia Dent Grant*, 1975.

Clouds and darkness surround us, yet Heaven is just, and the day of triumph will surely come, when justice & truth will be vindicated. Our wrongs will be made right, and we will once more, taste the blessings of freedom, of which the degraded rebels, would deprive us.

Mary Lincoln
Letter to James Gordon Bennett,
publisher of the *New York Herald*,
October 25, 1861.

I seem to be the scape-goat for both North and South.

Mary Lincoln
Letter to her half sister, Emilie Helm.

My husband, did the great work of the war, but Grant (now President), had all the pecuniary compensation.

> **Mary Lincoln**
> Letter to Rhoda White, May 23, 1871. [Since George Washington, the president's salary had been $25,000 a year; it was increased to $50,000 in 1871. Ulysses S. Grant became president in 1869.

Was there ever such a savage, wicked war?

> **Julia Gardiner Tyler**
> Letter to her mother, Juliana Gardiner, May 4, 1861.

Grover Cleveland

What a stone wall Cleveland is! My respect and admiration for him increase daily . . .

> **Ellen Axson Wilson**
> Letter to Woodrow Wilson, April 1, 1885.

Hillary Rodham Clinton

I think she should be allowed to make a choice. I'm not one for nit-picking.

> **Barbara Bush**
> Defending Hillary Clinton's career; press conference, Smithsonian's National Museum of American History, Washington, D.C., March 27, 1992.

William Jefferson Clinton

Hillary Rodham Clinton

You know, . . . Bill Clinton is going to be president of the United States someday!

Hillary Rodham Clinton
To co-worker Tom Bell while working in Washington, D.C., David Maraniss, *First In His Class*, 1995.

I'm sitting here because I love him, and I honor what he's been through, and what we've been through together, and you know, if that's not enough for people, then, heck, don't vote for him.

Hillary Rodham Clinton
Interview, *60 Minutes*, CBS-TV, January 26, 1992. Statement made during joint appearance with her husband after he had been accused of marital infidelity.

I think my husband has proven that he's a man who really cares about this country deeply and respects the presidency and believes strongly that he's doing the right thing. And when it's all said and done, that's how most fair-minded Americans will judge my husband. And all the rest of this stuff [accusations of President Clinton's misconduct] will end up in the garbage can where it deserves to be.

Hillary Rodham Clinton
Interview, *Reuters News Agency*, December 11, 1993.

Clothes

A little of what you call frippery is very necessary toward looking like the rest of the world.

Abigail Adams
Letter to John Adams, May 1, 1780.

So far as example goes, I shall bring in the use of silks. At my Age I think I am priviledged [sic] to set a fashion.

Abigail Adams
Letter to Mary Cranch,
November 26, 1799.

I went through my closets and drawers looking for a Swatch watch. I mean, after you've been on the Worst Dressed List, you will look for anything.

Hillary Rodham Clinton
Comments at White House reception
for the fashion industry,
September 19, 1994.

Imagine paying $800 or $900 for a dress! I'm perfectly happy with those little $17.95 numbers I order from New York newspaper ads.

Mamie Eisenhower
Comments when she was criticized
in the French press for preferring to
wear American clothes while living in
Paris when General Eisenhower
served as NATO commander,
1950–1952. Quoted, *Look*,
February 25, 1954.

As an American woman I have always valued my right to pretty clothes.

Mamie Eisenhower
Message supporting National Fashion
Press Week, January 3, 1952.

As a soldier's wife I learned early in life that pride in personal appearance is not a superficial thing. It rates high on every officer's efficiency report—and his family is part of that report. An Army wife sometimes has fewer dresses than her husband has uniforms. Consequently my training has been to select carefully and wear my clothes a long time. Knowing what to look for and how to tell a lasting fashion from a temporary fad has always helped me to shop intelligently.

Mamie Eisenhower
Comments to editors attending
National Fashion Press Week,
January 5, 1952.

I hate old-lady clothes and I shall never wear them.

Mamie Eisenhower
Quoted, Karal Ann Marling,
As Seen on T.V., 1994.

It is amusing to look on and see the great variety of costume, and the great effort made to rival each other at display in dress. But it does not interest me.

Abigail Fillmore
Comments written August 20, 1848,
after observing the clothes worn by
the "gay fashionable society," when
she was vacationing at Newport,
Rhode Island.

While I want them very nice, I don't want them very expensive.

Lou Henry Hoover
Letter to her mother, Florence Henry,
August 1899, expressing her reluctance
to spend a great deal of money on
her dresses.

. . . since I have lived here I'm well aware of how fast a costume is out of date.

Claudia Lady Bird Johnson
Comments introducing a fashion
show at the Governors' Wives
Luncheon, White House,
February 29, 1968.

I hate a full closet. I've gotten ruthless about what looks best on me. I don't have much chance to plod around the stores, but anybody in public life must be equipped with clothes in advance.

Jacqueline Kennedy
Interview, *The New York Times*,
September 15, 1960.

Just make sure no one has exactly the same dress I do. . . . I want all of mine to be original & no fat little woman hopping around in the same dress.

> **Jacqueline Kennedy**
> Letter to Oleg Cassini,
> December 13, 1960.

. . . wouldn't you rather wear your blue jeans than wander around in a hoop skirt?

> **Jacqueline Kennedy Onassis**
> Commenting on clothes worn by
> Russian nobility during a book lun-
> cheon, New York, January 13, 1977.

As you have everything that is beautiful and we have nothing—I will ask the favor of you to send me by safe vessels—large headdresses— a few flowers, feathers, gloves and stockings, black and white and any other pretty things suitable to an economist, and draw upon my husband for the amount.

> **Dolley Madison**
> Letter to Ruth Barlow, wife of the
> French minister, who was then in
> Paris, November 15, 1811.

I keep all my coats. My weight doesn't change.

> **Patricia Pat Nixon**
> News conference, Chicago,
> July 26, 1960.

It was necessary that I should be suitably dressed. Alas, alas, I had to pay $135. for it!

> **Edith Kermit Roosevelt**
> Letter to Amy Cheney, her husband's
> secretary, September 1901, lament-
> ing over the cost of a black dress she
> purchased for proper attire when she
> became First Lady following the
> assassination of President McKinley.

It is cold. I think I have to wear a velvet dress . . . the one that has two colors, blue and red.

Eleanor Roosevelt
Describing what she would wear to a formal reception. White House press conference, February 4, 1936.

I haven't any new clothes for Easter.

Eleanor Roosevelt
White House press conference, April 1, 1944.

Coffee and Tea

Personally, whether I drink coffee, tea or hot water, it is all the same to me.

Eleanor Roosevelt
White House press conference, discussing coffee rationing, November 24, 1942.

I find that black tea is better for me than coffee which I thought I never could live without. I have acquired a fondness for black tea and scarcely regret the coffee.

Julia Gardiner Tyler
Letter to her mother, Juliana Gardiner, June 17, 1845, attributing her recovery from a mild illness to the drinking of black tea.

Comments

I can't do that. I haven't done it in Washington.

Bess Truman
Reply to reporters asking her if she would speak for publication; New York, October 27, 1945.

Committees

. . . I have always felt that one should not go on committees if one is not prepared to be a working member . . .

Jacqueline Kennedy
> Letter to Congressman Carroll Deane, January 1961.

Complaints

I have made it my rule, not to repine—if all is not according to my wishes. I still have more than my desserts.

Abigail Adams
> Letter to William Shaw, January 6, 1799.

Conduct

Everyone is accountable for his conduct, and none is so insignificant as not to have some influence.

Abigail Adams
> Letter to her son Charles Adams; undated, apparently sent 1786.

Congress

Congress trifle away the most precious of their days . . .

Dolley Madison
> Letter to Hannah Gallatin, December 29, 1814, expressing her frustration over the lack of progress on peace settlement with Great Britain.

Conservation

The language of conservation is for me a language of love.

Claudia Lady Bird Johnson
Remarks at Conservation Luncheon,
White House, November 13, 1968.

Constitution

May the foundation of our new constitution, be justice, Truth and Righteousness. Like the wise Mans house may it be founded upon the Rocks and then neither storms or tempests will overthrow it.

Abigail Adams
Letter to John Adams, July 14, 1776.

Cook/Cooking

My cooking was and still is about the worst in America. George is so kind about it.

Barbara Bush
Former First Ladies Forum,
Kennedy Center, Washington, D.C.,
March 9, 1998.

I could cook a little but, I must confess, I was never a great success at this . . .

Grace Coolidge
*Grace Coolidge—
An Autobiography*, 1992.

. . . I am not a good cook.

Mamie Eisenhower
Telling reporters that her husband,
General Dwight D. Eisenhower, was
a better cook than she. Eisenhower
had been nominated as the
Republican Party's presidential
candidate. Chicago, July 13, 1952.

My principal want is a well disposed cook and if the characters of steward and cook cannot be blended in the same person, I would prefer the latter.

Martha Washington
Letter to Mrs. Elizabeth Powel,
May 1, 1797.

Cooperation

It seems to me . . . we have reached a place where it is not a question of "can we live in the same world and cooperate" but "we must live in the same world and learn to cooperate."

Eleanor Roosevelt
Letter to Queen Juliana of the
Netherlands, February 14, 1958.

Courage

We possess a spirit that will not be held conquered. If our men are all drawn off and we should be attacked, you will find a race of Amazons in America.

Abigail Adams
Letter to John Adams,
September 20, 1777.

I am not afraid of time or lies or defeat.

Claudia Lady Bird Johnson
Note written to her husband on
August 26, 1964, supporting
President Lyndon B. Johnson, who
had doubts about running for the
presidency in 1964.

Crime

The modern history of our own times furnishes as black a list of crimes as can be paralleled in ancient times . . .

Abigail Adams
Letter to John Quincy Adams,
June 1778.

Criticism

I expected to be vilified and abused with my whole family when I came into this situation [politics].

Abigail Adams
Letter to Mary Cranch, June 8, 1797.

Put a little wool in your ears and don't read the papers.

Louisa Adams
Advice to John Quincy Adams, when he was Secretary of State, and under attack by his political enemies.

The ugly scapegoating that divides our country is the problem, not the solution.

Barbara Bush
Comments while campaigning in Petersborough, New Hampshire, January 23, 1992.

The First Lady is going to be criticized no matter what she does. If she does too little. If she does too much. And I think you just have to be yourself and do the best you can. And so what? That's the way it is.

Barbara Bush
Former First Ladies Forum, Kennedy Center, Washington, D.C., March 9, 1998.

I told Hillary [Clinton] what I tell everybody in public life. You're going to be criticized no matter what you do, so be criticized for what you think is best and right for the country.

Rosalynn Carter
Address to Peace Links, a humanitarian group made up of Congressional wives, Washington, D.C., December 7, 1992.

This is one of the challenges I find hard. The level of criticism and attacks are astonishing to me, and some things are beyond pale, and your breath is taken away.

Hillary Rodham Clinton
Speaking to a class on presidential wives offered by the George Washington University, November 29, 1994.

If I'm going to be controversial I might as well be controversial on the things I really say.

Hillary Rodham Clinton
White House luncheon with women reporters, January 9, 1995.

I apparently remind some people of their mother-in-law or their boss, or something.

Hillary Rodham Clinton
Attempting to explain the level of animosity toward her. Quoted by Henry Louis Gates, Jr., *The New Yorker*, Combined Issue of February 26 and March 4, 1996.

While I'm grateful in a country as this to live among people who do disagree, to be critical of our government, to be critical of the political process, I have to confess, I get tired of hearing people blame every problem we have on the government.

Hillary Rodham Clinton
Commencement address, Drew University, Madison, New Jersey, May 18, 1996.

Not really; we do box it off. We have to box it off, because there is no way that you can let people with their own agendas, whatever they might be, interfere with your life, your private life or your public duties, and that's what my husband does every single day.

> **Hillary Rodham Clinton**
> Reply to a reporter's question whether the notoriety of the Paula Jones sexual harassment lawsuit against her husband had affected her life. Interview, Mutual-NBC Radio, January 19, 1998.

You know, I wouldn't say that it's not hard, because it is difficult and painful any time someone you care about, you love and you admire is attacked and subjected to such relentless accusations as my husband has been. But I also have now lived with this for, gosh, more than six years, and I have seen how these charges and accusations evaporate and disappear if they're ever given the light of day.

> **Hillary Rodham Clinton**
> Comments to reporters on allegations that her husband had an affair with a White House intern, White House, January 21, 1998.

If your husband is a political figure, you have to be thick-skinned. There's always going to be a lot of criticism. It comes with the office and you have to ignore it.

> **Betty Ford**
> Press interview after receiving the Hubert H. Humphrey Inspirational Award from the American Cancer Society, Washington, D.C., March 19, 1982.

I take long baths and carry on lengthy conversations with the person [who criticized her]. Of course, I always come out marvelously well in those conversations and I am able to say all the things I can't say aloud but long to.

> **Nancy Reagan**
> On overcoming criticism; quoted, *The New York Times*, March 21, 1972.

I have read a great deal about previous First Ladies who have all received it. It seems to go with the job.

> **Nancy Reagan**
> Her response to written questions
> about criticism, White House.
> October 12, 1981.

I shall likely be criticized. I cannot help it.

> **Eleanor Roosevelt**
> Remarks to her friend Lorena Hickok
> after Franklin Roosevelt was elected
> President, November 8, 1932.

After 25 years in politics, [I] have learned to accept it to a certain extent.

> **Bess Truman**
> Written reply to reporters asking if
> unfavorable criticism of the President
> disturbed her. White House,
> October 25, 1947.

My darling, I am not afraid of criticism . . .

> **Ellen Axson Wilson**
> Letter to Woodrow Wilson,
> undated, 1884.

Curiosity

I think, at a child's birth, if a mother could ask a fairy godmother to endow it with the most useful gift, that gift would be curiosity.

> **Eleanor Roosevelt**
> *Today's Health*, October 2, 1966.

Dancing

To dance in these rooms would be undignified, and it would be respectful neither to the house nor to the office.

Sarah Childress Polk
Denying permission for a party of young ladies to dance in the White House. Anson and Fanny Nelson, *Memorials of Sarah Childress Polk*, 1892.

Dawn

The dawn has come—and the hideous dark of the hour before the dawn has been lost in the gracious gift of light.

Edith Wilson
Letter to Woodrow Wilson, September 19, 1915.

Day Dreams

. . . my feelings & hopes are all so sanguine that in this dull world of reality tis [sic] best to dispel our delusive day dreams so soon as possible.

Mary Lincoln
Letter to Mercy Ann Levering, July 23, 1840.

Death

. . . they tell me that it was an act of the Almighty .. but oh, can anything compensate for the agony of this last sad parting on earth, after fifty years of union, without the privilege of indulging the feelings which all hold sacred at such moments.

> **Louisa Adams**
> Letter to her sister, Harriet Boyd, February 23, 1847. John Quincy Adams, who served 17 years in the House of Representatives after leaving the presidency, suffered a stroke on the floor of the House on February 21, 1847, and was carried to the Speaker's Room, where he died two days later.

Well, my dear, you are not going to die as I am here to nurse you back to life; so please do not speak again of death.

> **Lucretia Garfield**
> To her husband as he lay dying after being shot by an assassin July 2, 1881; he died September 19, 1881.

They can't hurt you now.

> **Florence Harding**
> Remarks to her dead husband in his coffin, August 2, 1923.

I hope my dear, you will always bear upon your mind that you are born to die and we know not how soon death may overtake us, it will be little consequence if we are rightly prepared for the event.

> **Anna Harrison**
> Letter to her son William, May 8, 1819.

All his bright light gone from the world.

> **Jacqueline Kennedy**
> Statement, thanking persons who had sent her messages of sympathy and grief over her husband's death. Washington, D.C., January 14, 1964.

Oh, my God, and have I given my husband to die.

Mary Lincoln
Her cry after President Lincoln was
assassinated at the Ford's Theater,
Washington, D.C., April 14, 1865.

To rejoin my Husband, who loved me so devotedly & whom I
idolized, would be bliss indeed.

Mary Lincoln
Letter to Oliver S. Halsted, Jr.,
May 29, 1865.

I felt & prayed—that my own appointed time, would not, be far distant.

Mary Lincoln
Letter to Mary Jane Welles,
December 29, 1865.

Death would be far more preferable to me, than my present life,
believe me—the young life of my Taddie, is all that makes life
endurable to me . . .

Mary Lincoln
Letter to Sally Orne,
November 14, 1869.

. . . the dear one grows still dearer even in death . . .

Jane Pierce
Letter to her sister Frances Packard,
February 1830, on the death of their
brother William Appleton.

. . . the story is over.

Eleanor Roosevelt
Comments to reporters when she
returned to Hyde Park after the
death of President Franklin D.
Roosevelt in 1945.

It is over now. I shall soon follow him. I have no more trials to pass through.

> **Martha Washington**
> Upon the death of her husband,
> George Washington,
> December 14, 1789.

For myself I have only to bow with humble submission to the will of that God who giveth and who taketh away looking forward with faith and hope to the moment when I shall be again united with the Partner of my life.

> **Martha Washington**
> Letter to Jonathan Trumbull,
> January 15, 1800.

Death Penalty

I think people would be alive today if there was a death penalty.

> **Nancy Reagan**
> Remarks after the assassination
> attempt on President Ronald Reagan,
> March 30, 1981.

I think the death penalty should be used against anybody who is proven to be responsible for a death.

> **Nancy Reagan**
> Interview, "Meet the Press," *NBC*,
> September 14, 1986.

I do not believe in capital punishment, but do believe that if it is the law it should be enforced wherever the case so demands.

> **Eleanor Roosevelt**
> Comments to reporters on the death
> sentence of Bruno Richard
> Hauptmann, convicted kidnapper
> and killer of the son of aviator
> Charles A. Lindbergh, New York,
> February 22, 1935.

Debts

Debts are my abhorrence. I never will borrow if any other method can be devised.

Abigail Adams
Letter to John Adams, July 15, 1778.

I always had a horror of debt.

Julia Dent Grant
The Personal Memoirs of Julia Dent Grant, 1975.

. . . I write to thank you, for your patience and soliciting as an especial favor to me, having been a punctual customer & always hoping to be so, a delay of the Settlement of my account with you, until the lst of June—when I promise, that without fail, then, the whole account shall be settled.

Mary Lincoln
Letter to A.T. Stewart, April 16, 1864. Mrs. Lincoln often amassed huge bills, especially for fashions, that she was unable to pay.

If he is re-elected I can keep him in ignorance of my affairs; but if he is defeated, then the bills will be sent in, and he will know all.

Mary Lincoln
To Elizabeth Keckley, White House seamstress and friend. As the 1864 election approached, Mrs. Lincoln revealed that she owed over $27,000 to New York stores for fashionable clothes.

Decisions

I asked not my Heart what it could, but what it ought to do.

Abigail Adams
Letter to Hannah Storer, March 1, 1778.

You know, you pay a price no matter what decision you make.

Hillary Rodham Clinton
Quoted by Henry Louis Gates, Jr.,
The New Yorker, Combined Issue of
February 26 and March 4,1996.

My husband makes his decisions. I might suggest an idea to him, but my husband makes his decisions.

Nancy Reagan
Quoted, *The New York Times
Magazine*, October 26, 1980.

So began my stewardship. [After President Wilson suffered a stroke in October 1919.] I studied every paper, sent from the different Secretaries or Senators, and tried to digest and present in tabloid form the things that, despite my vigilance, had to go to the President. I, myself, never made a single decision regarding the disposition of public affairs. The only decision that was mine was what was important and what was not, and the very important decision of when to present matters to my husband.

Edith Wilson
My Memoir, 1939.

Deeds

We want more men of deeds, and fewer of words . . .

Abigail Adams
Letter to William Smith,
June 10, 1797.

Defeat

It has never been possible to make me believe that defeat is a disgrace.

Louisa Adams
After John Quincy Adams was
defeated for reelection by Andrew
Jackson, 1828.

Democracy

In a democracy, government is the people, so renewing our faith in our government means renewing faith in ourselves and in our ability to perfect our union.

Hillary Rodham Clinton
Commencement address, Drew University, Madison, New Jersey, May 18, 1996.

. . . democracy is nurtured and sustained in the hearts of people, in the principles they honor, in the way they live their daily lives, and how they treat their fellow citizens and lessons they teach their children before they tuck them into bed at night.

Hillary Rodham Clinton
Speech, University of Ulster, Belfast, Northern Ireland, October 31, 1997.

Democracy can not flourish if women are not full partners in the social, economic, political and civil life of their communities and nations. Societies will only address the issues closest to the hearts of women when women themselves claim their rights as citizens.

Hillary Rodham Clinton
Speech, University of Ulster, Belfast, Northern Ireland, October 31, 1997.

Anybody got a better one? I haven't heard of any that I think are better, imperfect as this one is.

Claudia Lady Bird Johnson
Defending the American political system, television interview, *Group W. News*, November 11, 1973.

I . . . feel very strongly that we must set a good example of democracy at home if we are to be the leaders of the free world and enjoy the friendship and respect of the people.

Jacqueline Kennedy
Interview by Henry Fonda, *CBS-TV*, November 2, 1960.

There is a necessity in a democracy for an educated public opinion. A democracy means that everybody have responsibility of their government. We must not look at government as something to contribute to our particular interest, but as a means by which we, as individuals, may accomplish the best we can for the whole people.

Eleanor Roosevelt
Address to the Institute of Women's Professional Relations, New York, March 28, 1935.

I believe that democracy is based on the ability to make democracy serve the good of the majority of the people. If it can't do that, then it should not live.

Eleanor Roosevelt
Address at John Marshall College of Law, Jersey City, New Jersey, June 16, 1937.

The basic belief that makes any democracy is a belief in the rights of the individual. The only way I think to real understanding of the democratic way of life is to live it. Democracy is never static and its growth depends on our own attitude. Therefore, it is a constant adventure and a form of government that requires of every citizen a maximum of unselfish devotion.

Eleanor Roosevelt
Radio broadcast, *NBC*, August 31, 1940.

While in our democracy, I feel that Americans who believe in democracy should lead. While other beliefs must exist and I would fight for the rights of others to their beliefs, I must work with those who hold to the fundamental beliefs which I consider sound and true.

Eleanor Roosevelt
"Mrs. FDR Speaks," *The New Republic*, February 3, 1947.

Democratic Party

I am a Democrat and proud of it.

Claudia Lady Bird Johnson
Speech at luncheon by the Federated
Democratic Women of Ohio,
Columbus, Ohio,
September 18, 1964.

The Democrats today trust in the people, the plain, ordinary, everyday citizen, neither superlatively rich nor distressingly poor, not one of the "best minds" but the average mind. The Socialists believe in making the Government the people's master; the Republicans believe that the moneyed "aristocracy," the few great financial minds, should rule the Government; the Democrats believe that the whole people should govern.

Eleanor Roosevelt
Current History, January 1928.

I want unity above everything else, I want a party that will fight for the things that we know to be right at home and abroad.

Eleanor Roosevelt
Speech, Democratic National
Advisory Committee, New York, 1959.

Democratic Values

Democratic values are at risk when that balance [of power] shifts to the extremes: When government becomes too cumbersome or too restrictive. When the marketplace, which by definition knows the price of everything but the value of nothing, lures citizens into becoming merely consumers who care about satisfying their personal wants.

Hillary Rodham Clinton
Addressing a group of Australian
women at the Sydney Opera House,
November 1996.

Depression

There is no reason at all for just feeling sorry for ourselves over our present economic social problems. But there is every reason for each one of us to help solve the problem near us.

> **Lou Henry Hoover**
> Speech, Girl Scout convention,
> Buffalo, New York, August 1931.

I do not know the solution for these difficulties, but I know they require the same spirit which our ancestors showed when they founded this nation. It is a spirit which is not afraid of new difficulties and new solutions, nor afraid to stand hardships.

> **Eleanor Roosevelt**
> Speech, Congress of States Societies,
> New York, January 14, 1932.

The time is one that requires courage and common sense on everybody's part.

> **Eleanor Roosevelt**
> Statement at the first White House
> press conference ever held by a
> First Lady, March 6, 1933.

Desegregation

We have to desegregate housing before we desegregate schools.

> **Eleanor Roosevelt**
> Letter to Adlai Stevenson,
> June 13, 1956.

Desolation

Never, in my life, have I had the least idea, of the meaning of the word, *Desolation!*

Mary Lincoln
Letter to Elizabeth Blair Lee, July 11, 1865. Mrs. Lee was one of the few persons who remained her friend after President Lincoln's assassination.

Despondency

. . . I long to fly away sometimes, I hardly know when, only to freedom & quiet, but then seek to serve myself to head on in the path of duty and necessity . . .

Jane Pierce
Letter to Mary Aiken, June 1, 1853; expressing sadness over the loss of her son Benjamin (Benny).

Destiny

There is one secret, and that is the power we all have in forming our own destinies.

Dolley Madison
Letter to Mary Cutts, August 1, 1833.

Development

Our obligation to the world is primarily our obligation to our own future. Obviously, we cannot develop beyond a certain point unless other nations develop, too.

Eleanor Roosevelt
Remark on her 75th birthday, October 11, 1959.

Diary

Heavens no! It would get subpoenaed. I can't write anything down [laughing].

Hillary Rodham Clinton
Reply when asked by Jim Lehrer if
she kept a diary, *PBS Newshour,*
May 28, 1996.

Diplomacy

There is a small articulate minority in this country which advocates changing our national symbol which is the eagle to that of the ostrich and withdrawing from the United Nations.

Eleanor Roosevelt
Speech, Democratic National
Convention, July 1952.

We have to face the fact that either all of us are going to die together or we are going to learn to live together and if we are to live together we have to talk.

Eleanor Roosevelt
The New York Times,
October 15, 1960.

Disagreement

I feel compelled to disagree with him at times [but] I never have publicly disagreed with him and I have a very good reason for doing that. . . . I know Jimmy well and I think that if I made our disagreement public, I would lose all my effectiveness with him. I don't think it would help in any way to change his mind about anything.

Rosalynn Carter
Interview with Barbara Walters,
ABC-TV, December 12, 1978.

It is disagreeable to take stands. It was always easier to compromise, always easier to let things go. To many women, and I am one of them, it is extraordinarily difficult to care about anything enough to cause disagreement or unpleasant feelings, but I have come to the conclusion that this must be done for a time until we can prove our [political] strength and demand respect for our wishes.

> **Eleanor Roosevelt**
> Speech, state convention of the New York Democratic Party, Albany, New York, April 14, 1924.

Discipline

The thing we need to stress, . . . is the necessity for discipline, so that the material comforts which have come to us generally, will not make us soft.

> **Eleanor Roosevelt**
> Address, Wells College Alumnae Association, New York, March 29, 1932.

Discrimination

. . . I always tell them [young people] if they give up on their education and feel bad about themselves, then the person who [discriminates] wins and you lose. I don't think you look a loser to me.

> **Hillary Rodham Clinton**
> Comments to a young Gypsy who told her of discrimination; Budapest, Hungary, July 7, 1996.

I believe that it is essential to our leadership in the world and to the development of true democracy in our own country to have no discrimination in our country whatsoever. This is most important in the schools of our country.

> **Eleanor Roosevelt**
> Letter to Richard Bolling, January 20, 1956.

I deplore any action which denies artistic talent and opportunity to express itself because of prejudice against race or origin.

> **Bess Truman**
> Telegram, October 11, 1945, to Congressman Adam Clayton Powell of New York, who criticized her for accepting an invitation to a tea given by the Daughters of the American Revolution.
> The DAR had refused to allow Powell's wife, Hazel Scott, a black pianist, to perform in the DAR-owned Constitution Hall in Washington, D.C. Mrs. Truman attended the tea, and told Powell that, "In my opinion the acceptance of the hospitality is not related to the merits of the issue . . . "

Doctors

I think the doctors would especially like to keep one in bed. The love of money, is the root of all evil.

> **Mary Lincoln**
> Letter to Mary Harlan Lincoln, no date, probably 1870.

Domestic Training

Few girls receive domestic training these days. A girl may be a good stenographer, bookkeeper, law clerk or politician, but few know how to bake a cake, darn a sock or do any of the thousand-and-one little domestic tricks their grandmothers could perform as second nature.

> **Lou Henry Hoover**
> Speech, National Council of Girl Scouts Convention, Savannah, Georgia, January 26, 1922.

Drugs

Just say no!

Nancy Reagan
> Response when asked by school-
> children in Oakland, California, how
> they should resist peer pressure to
> take drugs, 1984. It became the
> motto for her anti-drug ampaign.

We have to have the fight against drugs, but I
don't believe that just dumping a lot of money
into this is going to solve the problem.

Nancy Reagan

Nancy Reagan
> Interview, "Meet the Press," *NBC*,
> November 14, 1986.

I'm saying that if you're a casual drug user, you are an accomplice to
murder.

Nancy Reagan
> Address at White House Conference
> for a Drug Free America,
> February 29, 1988.

It is the United States alone which bears responsibility for its own
drug problem. I am not blaming other nations. While most of the ille-
gal drugs are imported, the drug users are home-grown.

Nancy Reagan
> Address to the General Assembly of
> the United Nations,
> October 25, 1988.

It is often easier to make strong speeches about foreign drug lords or
drug smugglers than to arrest a pair of Wall Street investment bankers
buying cocaine on their lunch break.

Nancy Reagan
> Address to the General Assembly of
> the United Nations,
> October 25, 1988.

Economics

Whatever tends to establish our people on a sound economic basis must be of utmost interest to women, for they are the makers of household budgets, the managers of the homes, which in the final analysis are the end and aim of organized society. They direct most of the spending, and on them fall large responsibilities of those measures of thrift, economy and careful expenditure which greatly concern the welfare of our country's and the world affairs.

Forence Harding
Letter to the Southern Tariff
Association, January 18, 1921.

Education

If we mean to have Heroes, Statesmen and Philosophers, we should have learned women. . . . If much depends as is allowed upon the early Education of youth and the first principals which are instilled take the deepest root, great benefit must arise from literary accomplishments in women.

Abigail Adams
Letter to John Adams,
August 14, 1776.

. . . I hope more parents will become involved in their children's education.

Barbara Bush
"Our Reading Problem," Op-ed
article she wrote for *The Washington Post*, August 2, 1984.

Education brings learning, but it is useless unless it also brings a courageous attitude toward life.

Claudia Lady Bird Johnson
Speech, Georgetown Visitation
Preparatory School, Washington,
D.C., June 3, 1964.

Education is the most lasting investment anyone can make.

Claudia Lady Bird Johnson
Speech to the women's branch of
the Union of Orthodox Jewish
Congregations, Washington, D.C.,
November 23, 1966.

Teachers cannot teach alone; students cannot learn alone; education
must be a family affair.

Claudia Lady Bird Johnson
Remarks at the Parent-Child Project,
Glenwood Elementary School,
Charleston, West Virginia,
March 13, 1967.

Education should develop two things—skill of mind and skill of hand.

Eleanor Roosevelt
Speech, Cornell University, Ithaca,
New York, October 23, 1937.

First and foremost, we must have whatever rights of citizenship are
ours under the Constitution. Then we must have education for
everybody.

Eleanor Roosevelt
Speech, national conference of the
National Association for the
Advancement of Colored People
(NAACP), Richmond, Virginia,
July 2, 1939.

A democratic form of government, a democratic way of life,
presupposes free public education over a long period; it presupposes
also an education for personal responsibility that too often is neglected.

Eleanor Roosevelt
"Let Us Have Faith in Democracy,"
Department of Agriculture *Land
Policy Review*, January 1942.

Mamie Eisenhower

She is an inspiration to the country and to me. I have admired her never-failing companionship with her husband.

> **Claudia Lady Bird Johnson**
> Comments after visiting Mrs. Mamie Eisenhower, Washington, D.C., March 29, 1969.

Election

I don't want you to have the nomination merely because no one else can get it. I want you to have it when the whole country calls for you . . .

> **Lucretia Garfield**
> Letter to James A. Garfield, June 4, 1880. Four days later Garfield was nominated to be the Republican Party's candidate for president.

Endurance

. . . while women may not have as much muscular strength as men, they have as much endurance and ability to bear strain as the male of the species.

> **Eleanor Roosevelt**
> Radio broadcast, *NBC*, September 4, 1934.

English Language

. . . every single American citizen should have to speak and understand English—otherwise they will become second-class citizens.

> **Barbara Bush**
> Interview, *The New York Times*, April 8, 1984.

Unless you speak English and read well, you'll never be a first-class citizen . . . but when you say "official," that becomes a racial slur.

> **Barbara Bush**
> Quoted, *USA Today*,
> October 15, 1990.

Nobody is going to suceed in this country unless you speak English well. I am unapologetic about that because I think it's unfair to students to do otherwise.

> **Hillary Rodham Clinton**
> Comments at the Washington Post
> Principals Leadership Institute,
> Washington, D.C., July 1, 1997.

Entertaining

During the day I'll work on health care. During the night I'm going to have fun. . . . I want no serious talk. I don't want any business. I want fun.

> **Hillary Rodham Clinton**
> On her plans for a Congressional
> Ball, interview, *The Washington Post*,
> November 24, 1993.

I was more proficient in setting up and operating miniature tracks and trains on the dining room floor than in receiving and entertaining guests in the drawing room.

> **Grace Coolidge**
> *Grace Coolidge—An Autobiography*,
> 1992.

I want people to enjoy themselves in the manner that is most pleasing to them.

> **Lucy Hayes**
> While Mrs. Hayes barred the serving
> of alcohol in the White House, she
> did not wish to dictate to others on
> the use of wine and spirits.

I may perhaps surprise you when I mention that I am recovering from the slight fatigue of a very large and I really believe a very handsome entertainment, at least our friends flatter us by saying so. About five hundred were invited, yet owing to an unlucky rain three hundred only favored us by their prescence . . .

Mary Lincoln
Letter to her sister Emilie Todd Helm,
February 15, 1856.

I will go out with my Dearest and enjoy it.

Ida Saxton McKinley
Diary, April 15, 1901.

Yesterday we had ninety persons to dine with us at one table . . . I am less worried here [Montpelier, Virginia] with an hundred visitors than with twenty-five in Washington . . .

Dolley Madison
Letter to her sister, Anna Payne Cutts,
July 5, 1820.

. . . have you not lived in Washington long enough to know that the cooks fix the hour for dinner?

Sarah Childress Polk
Reply to a guest who had expected
to be served dinner at 6 o'clock.
Anson and Fanny Nelson, *Memorials
of Sarah Childress Polk*, 1892.

What dinner parties of the usual kind in country or city would not appear dull to me after all those brilliant ones we gave at the White House!

Julia Gardiner Tyler
Letter to her mother, Juliana
Gardiner, no date, circa
May 15, 1845.

Environment

I've had a long love affair with the environment. It is my sustenance, my pleasure, my joy. Flowers in a city are like lipstick on a woman—it just makes you look better to have a little color.

Claudia Lady Bird Johnson
Time, September 5, 1989.

Envy

When I saw the large steamers at the New York landings I felt in my heart inclined to sigh that poverty was my portion. How I long to go to Europe. I often laugh and tell Mr. Lincoln that I am determined my next husband shall be rich.

Mary Lincoln
Letter to her sister Emilie Todd Helm, September 20, 1857.

Equality

Is it reasonable that the same number of stitches equally good should be worth less because taken by woman's weaker hand? Is it equitable that the woman who teaches school equally well should receive a smaller compensation than man, who is so much more able to support himself in other ways?

Lucretia Garfield
From an essay, titled "Women's Station," she wrote as a college student, September 18, 1851.

I really believe people should be equal.

Patricia Pat Nixon
Helen Thomas, *Dateline: White House*, 1975.

Surely it is better, and far more befitting the democratic ideals of this country, to make no distinction, and to have all women who wish to show their belief in preparedness march together on a basis of equality.

Edith Kermit Roosevelt
Letter to *The New York Times*, May 4, 1916, attacking criticism of women who were to participate in a citizen's preparedness parade. Mrs. J. Borden Harriman also signed the letter.

I believe in equal wages for men and women for equal work.

Eleanor Roosevelt
Address before Town Hall public forum, Washington, D.C., February 2, 1936.

I am sorry that governments in all parts of the world have not seen fit to send more women as delegates, alternates or advisors to the [United Nations] Assembly. I think it is in these positions that the women of every nation should work to see that equality exists.

Eleanor Roosevelt
Ladies' Home Journal, January 28, 1946.

I believe we will have better government when men and women discuss public issues together and make their decisions on the basis of their differing areas of concern for the welfare of their families and their world. Too often the great decisions are originated and given form in bodies made up wholly of men, or so completely dominated by them that whatever of special value women have to offer is shunted aside without expression.

Eleanor Roosevelt
Speech, United Nations, December 1952.

Equal Rights

I want equal rights for women, men, everybody, equal rights for every American, equal pay for equal work.

> **Barbara Bush**
> Quoted, *The Washington Post*,
> January 15, 1989.

The Equal Rights Amendment . . . will not alter the fabric of the Constitution—or force women away from their families.

> **Betty Ford**
> Speech, Greater Cleveland
> International Woman's Year
> Congress, October 25, 1975.

Women have equal rights if they want to exercise them. . . . I just don't feel there's any discrimination.

> **Patricia Pat Nixon**
> Comments to reporters, White House,
> May 7, 1969.

In this country we should all have, certainly, equal rights, and minorities should certainly have those exactly as majorities have them.

> **Eleanor Roosevelt**
> Speech at meeting of the New York
> Crisis Committee, New York,
> October 22, 1937.

Experience

Each generation must learn by its own experience, and though it may be hard to watch our children go through the same mistakes which we went through, it will do no good to pursue them with warnings. All we can do is to be worthy of their confidence.

> **Eleanor Roosevelt**
> Radio talk, *NBC*,
> January 27, 1933.

Face-lift

Not that I'm against it. It's just that I haven't needed it. At least I don't think I have.

Nancy Reagan
Quoted, *Parade*, January 18, 1981.

Facial

. . . never had a facial in my life, because I have never had time.

Eleanor Roosevelt
Press conference, January 31, 1939.

Fad

Oh, I know you think I'm boasting, but I have only one fad, the only fad I have had for the last twenty-six years, and that is my husband.

Florence Harding
Comments to reporters, National Republican Convention, Chicago, June 12, 1920.

Fairness

Americans are smart, fair-minded, savvy people.

Hillary Rodham Clinton
Appraising the public's reaction to a scandal involving her husband. Press conference, White House, February 11, 1998.

Fairy Tales

I have always had a passion for fairy tales . . .

> **Edith Kermit Roosevelt**
> Letter to Theodore Roosevelt,
> June 8, 1886.

Faith

We're both very fortunate that the way we were raised gave us a lot of resilience. I think our religious faith, our love and support for each other, and the friends and family that we have just enable us to see what we believe to be true and real and to make the distinction about what isn't.

> **Hillary Rodham Clinton**
> Describing how she and her husband
> weather controversies. Interview,
> *Mutual-NBC Radio*,
> January 19, 1998.

I believe that with enough faith in God you can face anything. I feel that very strongly.

> **Betty Ford**
> *McCall's*, February 1975.

I should not blame my own heart if it lost all faith in you.

> **Lucretia Garfield**
> Letter to James A. Garfield, July 7,
> 1867, when she learned that her
> husband was seeing another woman.

Faithfulness

I don't think there are many men who are faithful to their wives.
Men are such a combination of good and evil.

Jacqueline Kennedy
Remark made early in her marriage
to John F. Kennedy. Quoted in Peter
Collier and David Horowitz, *The
Kennedys: An American Drama*, 1984.

Family

Family is and must ever be the secondary consideration to a
zealous Patriot.

Louisa Adams
Upon learning that her husband,
former President John Quincy Adams,
was seeking election to Congress.

We get enormous strength from our family. Not just our children and
grandchildren, but our brothers and sisters. It's always been like that.
And more so now. Once you're in a position where you're really isolated from people, you count more heavily on your children and
your closest friends.

Barbara Bush
Press conference, Washington, D.C.,
January 14, 1989.

In our family, we've always done everything together.

Rosalynn Carter
Interview, *U.S. News & World
Report*, October 18, 1976.

When women are empowered to make the most of their own poten-
tial then their families will thrive, and when families thrive communities thrive and nations will thrive as well.

Hillary Rodham Clinton
Speech, University of Ulster, Belfast,
Northern Ireland, October 31, 1997.

Boys, remember you are just as great factors in the home making of the family as are the girls. And remember, too, that the spirit of your contribution is of greater worth than the material value of it.

Lou Henry Hoover
Radio speech, *NBC*, to 4-H Boys and Girls Clubs, June 22, 1929.

Farming

If you will come home and turn farmer I will be dairy woman [and] we will grow wealthy.

Abigail Adams
Letter to John Adams, July 23, 1777.

Fatalism

Abigail Adams

Have you perceived anything like fatalism in my letters? I am unconscious of it, though I fear there may sometimes be a little inclination toward it.

Louisa Adams
Letter to her father-in-law, John Adams, April 16, 1819.

I don't know whether I believe in a future life . . . I came to feel that it didn't really matter very much because whatever the future held you'd have to face it when you came to it, just as whatever life holds you have to face it exactly the same way. I think I am pretty much a fatalist . . .

Eleanor Roosevelt
"This I Believe," *CBS* radio broadcast, 1951.

Father

After I lost my father I felt differently toward the President [John Tyler]. He seemed to fill the place and to be more agreeable in every way than any younger man ever was or could be.

Julia Gardiner Tyler
Philadelphia Press, July 11, 1889.

Favor

I thought that as wife of the President I was entitled to ask for so small a favor.

Mary Lincoln
Remark to Secretary of War Edwin M. Stanton after he had denied her request that a "strong Union man" be given a commissary, December 1864. Mrs. Lincoln quickly apologized, promising "never to ask for anything again."

Fear

I would like . . . to see us take hold of ourselves, look at ourselves and cease being afraid.

Eleanor Roosevelt
The New York Times,
October 12, 1954.

Feminism

Even though I am a feminist, I would never not put first my marriage and my family.

Betty Ford
Quoted by James Cannon in *Time and Change: Gerald Ford's Appointment With History*, 1994.

Feminism is the ability to choose what you want to do. I'm choosing what I want to do.

Nancy Reagan
McCall's, November 1985.

So—against odds, the women inch forward, but I'm rather old to be carrying on this fight!

Eleanor Roosevelt
Letter to Joseph P. Lash,
February 13, 1946.

Fight

. . . [I] have always been an advocate for fighting when assailed, though a Quaker.

Dolley Madison
Letter to her cousin, Edward Coles,
May 12, 1813.

I would rather fight with my hands than with my tongue.

Dolley Madison
Quoted by her grandniece, Lucia
Beverly Cutts, *Memoirs and Letters of
Dolly Madison*, 1886.

Finances

. . . I was raised to believe that every person had an obligation to take care of themselves and their family. And that meant, you know, earning an income and saving and investing.

Hillary Rodham Clinton
Press conference, White House,
April 22, 1994.

First Lady

You don't run for First Lady. . . . If they had a beauty contest, I would not win. If they had a contest for the wife with the best candidate, I would win.

Barbara Bush
Atlanta Constitution, May 29, 1988.

. . . the wife of the President of the United States is probably the most spoiled woman in the world.

Barbara Bush
Press conference, White House, January 16, 1990.

Well, I have enormous respect for every First Lady. I know you all think it's a cinch, but if you love your man and he's criticized a lot, and every one of them have had that, it's not so easy.

Barbara Bush
Comments after viewing a First Ladies exhibit at the Smithsonian's National Museum of American History, Washington, D.C., March 27, 1992.

I have learned that I have influence. I can look at a program and it gets some attention . . . [I feel] I have a responsibility to do that.

Rosalynn Carter
Interview, *Over Easy*, February 15, 1980.

I've enjoyed being a hostess.

Rosalynn Carter
Interview, *The Washington Post*, November 19, 1980.

I won't say that it's a relief not to be First Lady because I enjoyed every minute of it. I never did consciously weigh my words, but you do have to be very careful.

> **Rosalynn Carter**
> Comments at book luncheon,
> Washington, D.C., April 12, 1984.

Americans know that women are going to work. They don't mind if women work. They think it's nice for women to have leadership positions—I think they really do—but they think the First Lady ought to sit in the White House and take care of the President. I cannot understand that.

> **Rosalynn Carter**
> Address to Peace Links, a humanitarian group made up of Congressional wives, Washington, D.C., December 7, 1992.

First ladies have enormous influence just because of their proximity to power.

> **Rosalynn Carter**
> *Helping Yourself Help Others*, 1994.

The American people have made the role of the First Lady one of the most important jobs in the country. It happened because each First Lady from Martha Washington onward contributed to her husband's historical reputation. It is a tribute to American women that, coming from different social and economic backgrounds, from many different geographical regions, and with diverse educational preparation, each First Lady served our country so well. Each left her own mark, and each teaches us something special about our history.

> **Hillary Rodham Clinton**
> Introduction to *The First Ladies*, 1994 edition, published by The White House Historical Association.

And I think that, having been independent, having made decisions, it's a little difficult for us as a country, maybe, to make the transition of having a woman like many of the women [female reporters] in this room sitting in this house [White House]. So I think that the standards, and to some extent . . . the expectations and the demands have changed, and I'm trying to find my way through it and trying to figure out how best to be true to myself and how to fulfill my responsibilities to my husband and my daughter and the country.

Hillary Rodham Clinton
Press conference, White House,
April 22, 1994.

I'm often asked if what I am doing in Washington creates a new role model for first ladies. And I always say I don't want to create any new stereotype. I want to free women to live according to their own needs and desires. I do not want to create a new category that anyone after me must somehow fit into. I want all women to be given the respect they deserve to have for the choices they may make.

Hillary Rodham Clinton
Address, Scripps College, Claremont,
California, April 26, 1994.

I am surprised at the way people seem to perceive me, and sometimes I read stories and hear things about me that I go "ugh." I wouldn't like her either. It's so unlike what I think I am or what my friends think I am. So I can only guess that people are getting perceptions about me from things I am saying or doing in ways that don't correspond with things I am trying to get across. I didn't get this whole image-creation thing. I see what it can do, but I'm not sure I get it. I have let other people define me.

Hillary Rodham Clinton
Lunch with female writers, White
House, January 9, 1995.

This position is such an odd one. In our country we expect so much from the woman who is married to the President—but we don't really know what it is we expect. So I think there really is no way to escape the politics of one's time other than to just totally withdraw, perhaps, I don't know, have a bag over your head when you come out into the public or somehow make it clear that you have no opinion and no ideas about anything—and never express them, publicly or privately. There is something about the position itself which raises in Americans' minds concerns about hidden power, about influence behind the scenes, about unaccountability. Yet if you try to be public about your concerns and your interests, then that is equally criticized. I think the answer is to just be who you are and do what you can do and get through it—and wait for a First Lady to hold the position.

Hillary Rodham Clinton
Speaking to a group of Australian women at the Sydney Opera House, November 1996.

We New England women cling to the old way, and being the President's wife isn't going to make me think less about the domestic things I've always loved.

Grace Coolidge
Quoted by Ishbel Ross, *Grace Coolidge and Her Era*, 1962.

Being the wife of a government worker is a very confining position.

Grace Coolidge
Letter to a friend.

Grace Coolidge   It is difficult to describe my feelings [upon entering the White House] . . . this was I and yet not I, this was the wife of the President of the United States and she took precedence over me; my personal likes and dislikes must be subordinated to the consideration of those things which were required of her. . . .

Grace Coolidge
American Magazine,
September 1929.

Of course, being mistress of the White House is a terrific responsibility, and I am truly grateful for my Army wife training.

Mamie Eisenhower
Letter to reporter Nanette Kutner,
November 15, 1952.

[On becoming First Lady] . . . like being thrown into a river without knowing how to swim.

Betty Ford
McCall's, October 1974.

I don't feel that because I'm First Lady, I'm any different from what I was before. It can happen to anyone. After all, it has happened to anyone.

Betty Ford
The New York Times Magazine,
December 8, 1974.

I do not believe that being First Lady should prevent me from expressing my views . . .

Betty Ford
Speech, International Women's Year
Congress, Cleveland, 1975.

I had no idea when we came a year ago how many responsibilities there would be and decisions to be made as First Lady. I found that it was practically a seven-day-week, twenty-four-hour-a-day job.

Betty Ford
Comments on her first year in the
White House, news conference,
August 4, 1975.

Well, I never have been overawed by the position of First Lady. In fact, it's very hard for me to consider the concept in my own mind that I am the First Lady. So that was not a difficult situation for me. I did tell my husband when he was sworn in as President that I couldn't change. I would have to remain my same personality.

Betty Ford
Interview, *U.S. News & World
Report*, October 18, 1976.

If I had known that this was going to happen to me, I would have changed my nose and nickname.

Claudia Lady Bird Johnson
Remarks to Abigail McCarthy,
November 1963.

. . . my role must emerge in deeds, not words.

Claudia Lady Bird Johnson
The New York Times,
December 8, 1963.

I have learned something about the job of being the President's wife. She is not chosen by anyone except her husband and she really has no obligations except to him.

Claudia Lady Bird Johnson
Remarks at the Women's National
Press Club dinner, Washington, D.C.,
December 2, 1968.

There's no reason why one First Lady should have to be interested in painting china because another had this particular interest. There is no reason why, because I planted trees, another First Lady should have to water them. (Of course I hope someone will!)

Claudia Lady Bird Johnson
Remarks at the Women's National
Press Club dinner, Washington, D.C.,
December 2, 1968.

You come to know your country more, in depth, in a rare and wonderful way. And you wind up more in love with it than you ever were.

Claudia Lady Bird Johnson
On the pleasures of being a First
Lady, interview, *The New York Times,*
December 27, 1968.

The first lady is, and always has been, an unpaid public servant elected by one person, her husband.

Claudia Lady Bird Johnson
U.S. News & World Report,
March 9, 1972.

. . . it was just the most violent and awful beginning, and I sensed that I had walked on stage for a role I had never rehearsed . . .

Claudia Lady Bird Johnson
On becoming First Lady. Oral history interview, Lyndon Baines Johnson Library, January 23, 1987.

. . . I really got to know this country so much better and really the main result was just that it increased my faith and optimism about the country.

Claudia Lady Bird Johnson
On being First Lady, oral history interview, Lyndon Baines Johnson Library, October 10, 1990.

I think the major role of the First Lady is to take care of the President so that he can best serve the people. And not to fail her family, her husband, and children.

Jacqueline Kennedy
Interview with Charles Collingwood, CBS "Person-to-Person," September 29, 1960.

Well, of course, she can't expect to be a completely private person. She will have an official role which she must play and accept with grace . . .

Jacqueline Kennedy
Interview with Charles Collingwood, CBS "Person-to-Person," September 29, 1960.

I have always thought that the main duty [of the First Lady] is to preserve the President of the United States so he can be of best service to his country, and that means running a household smoothly around him, and helping him in any way he might ask you to.

Jacqueline Kennedy
Interview, Today TV show, September 15, 1960.

I really do not think of myself as the First Lady, but as Jack as President. . . . I assume I won't fail him in any way.

Jacqueline Kennedy
Comments at first press conference
after her husband was elected
President; Hyannis Port,
Massachusetts, November 10, 1960.

The one thing I do not want to be called is First Lady. It sounds like a saddle horse. Would you notify the telephone operators and everyone else that I'm to be known simply as Mrs. Kennedy and not as First Lady.

Jacqueline Kennedy
Instructions to her secretary following
her husband's inauguration as
President, January 20, 1961. Quoted
in Peter Collier and David Horowitz,
The Kennedys: An American Drama,
1984.

I'm taking the veil. I've had it with being First Lady all the time, and now I'm going to give more attention to my children. I want you to cut off all outside activity—whether it's a glass of sherry with a poet or a coffee with a king. No more art gallery dedications—no nothing —unless absolutely necessary.

Jacqueline Kennedy
Feeling the pressures of her position,
Mrs. Kennedy wrote this memo to
her social secretary on
January 11, 1963.

I think the major role of the First Lady is to take care of the President . . .

Jacqueline Kennedy
Quoted in Theodore C. Sorenson,
Kennedy, 1965.

You can imagine me the very shadow of my husband.

Dolley Madison
Letter to Mr. and Mrs. Barlow, 1811.

I just want to go down in history as the wife of the President.

Patricia Pat Nixon
Statement, 1970.

Being the First Lady is the hardest unpaid job in the world.

Patricia Pat Nixon
Interview in Monrovia, Liberia,
March 15, 1972.

[The most important role for a First Lady was] to take care of your husband so that he can be the best possible president.

Jacqueline Kennedy Onassis
Quoted by Ruth Montgomery, *Hail to the Chiefs*, 1970.

I admire all the first ladies.

Nancy Reagan
On role models, interview, *The Washington Post*,
November 21, 1980.

If the President has a bully pulpit, then the First Lady has a white glove pulpit. It is more refined, perhaps, more restricted, more ceremonial, but it's a bully pulpit all the same.

———

I suspect there are those who think first ladies should be kept in attics, only to say our lines, pour our tea and then be put away again.

Nancy Reagan
Speech, annual Associated Press luncheon for the Publishers Association,
Washington, D.C., May 4, 1987.

I see the First Lady as another means to keep a president from becoming isolated.

Nancy Reagan
International Herald Tribune, Paris,
May 26, 1988.

I think it's an important, legitimate role for a First Lady to look after a President's health and well being. And if that interferes with other plans, so be it. No first lady need to make apologies for looking out for her husband's personal welfare . . . .The First Lady is, first of all, a wife.

Nancy Reagan
Speech to members of a gas industry conference, Washington, D.C., June 9, 1988.

For eight years I was sleeping with the President. If that doesn't give you special access, I don't know what does.

Nancy Reagan
CBS, 60 Minutes, October 15, 1989.

Being in centre of things is very interesting, yet the same proportions remain. When I read "The World is too much with us" or "Oh for a closer walk with God" they mean just what they did, so I don't believe I have been forced into the "first lady of the land" model of my predecessors.

Edith Kermit Roosevelt
Letter to Cecil Spring-Rice, January 27, 1902.

. . . but there isn't going to be any First Lady. There is just to be plain, ordinary Mrs. Roosevelt . . . . I never wanted to be the president's wife, and I don't want it now. You don't quite believe me, do you? Very likely no one would—except possibly some woman who had had the job.

Eleanor Roosevelt
Quoted by Lorena Hickok, November 9, 1932.

You must live up to the standards just as any other first ladies have done and will do . . . . The First Lady is a little like the prisoner of history in the White House.

Eleanor Roosevelt
"Mrs. Eleanor Roosevelt's Own Radio Program," *NBC*, May 2, 1940.

You will feel that you are no longer clothing yourself. You are dressing a public monument.

Eleanor Roosevelt
On the role of the president's wife.
Quoted, *New York Herald Tribune*,
October 27, 1960.

Of course, there was objection . . . but I had my way and in spite of protests took my place at my husband's side.

Helen Taft
Recollections of Full Years, 1914.
On her insistence that she ride back
to the White House in President
Taft's limousine following his inau-
gural at the Capitol. Previously, the
outgoing President had ridden with
the new occupant back to the White
House. Since Theodore Roosevelt
had left Washington when the inau-
gural ceremonies ended, Mrs. Taft
decided to do something no First
Lady had done before, ride with her
presidential husband back to the
White House.

Good health and a well-developed sense of humor. Skill in public speaking would be very helpful.

Bess Truman
Written reply to reporters asking
what qualities would be the greatest
assets of the wife of the president.
White House, October 29, 1947.

I live a very dull life here [New York] and know nothing that passes in the town. I never go to any public place—indeed, I am more like a state prisoner than anything else. There is certain bounds set for me which I must not depart from—and as I cannot do as I like, I am obstinate, and stay at home a great deal.

Martha Washington
Letter to her niece, Frances Fanny
Bassett Washington,
October 23, 1789.

I sometimes think the arrangement is not quite as it ought to have been, that I, who had much rather be at home, should occupy a place with which a great many younger and gayer women would be prodigiously pleased.

Martha Washington
Letter to Mercy Otis Warren,
December 26, 1789.

. . . the practice of calling the President's wife the "First Lady" was always a disagreeable one to me. I think that if some clever person would start a little crusade against it in the newspapers it would be ridiculed to death.

Edith Wilson
My Memoir, 1939.

Fishing

I can fish, and do everything that goes with fishing, but I hate it all.

Eleanor Roosevelt
Comments upon returning from a
family fishing trip, April 11, 1934.

Flattery

This new experience of having people want to name things after us is really quite flattering until you realize they usually do it for people who are very, very old or dead.

Barbara Bush
Upon learning that a new Mesa,
Arizona school will be named the
Barbara Bush Elementary School.,
November 1995.

Flirtation

. . . I like Mr. Calhoun the best. . . . We had together a pleasant flirtation.

Julia Gardiner Tyler
Letter to her mother, Juliana
Gardiner, November 27, 1844,
describing a Washington banquet
where she found herself seated
between Secretary of State John C.
Calhoun and Attorney General
John Nelson.

Flowers

There is something remarkably more beautiful about flowers that you yourself have planted, and divided, and cared for, than any other flowers. It reminds one that the creation of beauty is a happy experience. I loved that time.

Claudia Lady Bird Johnson
Interview, *U.S. News & World
Report*, February 22, 1965.

We have the most beautiful flowers & grounds imaginable . . .

Mary Lincoln
Letter to Hannah Shearer,
July 11, 1861.

My favourite flower was, and is, the orchid; and knowing this, all through our friendship and engagement the President had sent orchids to me. I had worn them so constantly that they were known as "my" flower.

Edith Wilson
My Memoir, 1939.

Flying

I am not afraid [but] I promised my husband that I would never fly.

Grace Coolidge
To Charles A. Lindbergh after he
offered to take her for an airplane
ride. Lindbergh met the Coolidges
after his successful solo flight from
New York to Paris in May 1927.

Foreign Policy

We must be willing to learn that cooperation may imply compromise, but if it brings a world advance it is a gain for each individual nation.

Eleanor Roosevelt
Speech, Pilgrim Society,
January 21, 1946.

Forgiveness

Life is filled with the necessity for forgiveness.

Hillary Rodham Clinton
Press conference, New York,
July 11, 1992.

I should not let a mere word hurt me and so, by reaction, hurt you. I will try hard to be more sensible.

Ellen Axson Wilson
Forgiving her husband for some
carelessly spoken words; letter to
Woodrow Wilson,
September 4, 1913.

Formality

My experience is that the most formal branch of the government service is the naval branch. The state department may be as formal, but I doubt it.

Helen Taft
Recollections of Full Years, 1914.

Fortitude

. . . you have frequently endeavoured to teach me fortitude. I knew not then how much I should need it.

Luisa Adams
Letter to John Quincy Adams,
July 24, 1796.

Benjamin Franklin

I found him social, but not talkative, and when he spoke something useful dropped from his tongue; he was grave, yet pleasant, and affable.

Abigail Adams
Letter to John Adams,
November 5, 1775.

Frankness

In my usual vocal way, I've always told everybody that [what] I was going to do.

Betty Ford
Los Angeles Times,
November 12, 1995.

It really never occurred to me to simply ignore questions I didn't like. No one ever trained me to do that. I wish sometimes someone had.

> **Betty Ford**
> *Los Angeles Times,*
> November 12, 1995.

Freedom

Let me be clear: Freedom means the right of people to assemble, organize and debate openly. It means respecting the views of those who may disagree with the views of their governments. It means not taking citizens away from their loved ones and jailing them, mistreating them or denying them their freedom or dignity because of the peaceful expression of their ideas and opinions.

> **Hillary Rodham Clinton**
> Speech, United Nations Fourth
> World Conference on Women,
> Beijing, China, September 5, 1995.

. . . what does freedom mean if people remain imprisoned by their own bitterness?

> **Hillary Rodham Clinton**
> Speech, University of Ulster, Belfast,
> Northern Ireland, October 31, 1997.

To them [the nation's fathers] in this crisis we dedicate our lives . . . never to fall back in our purpose to leave to our children, and to our children's children, the freedom of life and thought which has been ours. For if we fail, we fall like Lucifer, never to hope again.

> **Edith Kermit Roosevelt**
> Speech, National Conference of
> Republican Women,
> September 16, 1935.

Certain rights can never be granted to the government, but must be kept in the hands of the people.

> **Eleanor Roosevelt**
> *The New York Times,* May 3, 1948.

Freedom of Speech

As women are not masons, or bound to keep secrets, they are entitled to a greater latitude of speech than Men.

> **Abigail Adams**
> Letter to William Shaw,
> December 21, 1798.

We must always uphold the idea of our colleges as incubators of
ideas and havens for free speech and free thought. . . . Freedom and
respect are not values that should be in conflict with each other. . . .
We must be careful not to cross the line between censuring behavior
we consider unacceptable and censoring. We have to believe that in
the free exchange of ideas, justice will prevail over injustice, tolerance over intolerance and progress over reaction.

> **Hillary Rodham Clinton**
> Commencement address, University
> of Pennsylvania, Philadelphia,
> May 17, 1993.

For the first time in my life I can say just what I want. For your information it is wonderful to feel free.

> **Eleanor Roosevelt**
> Comments to reporters as she
> embarked for London on the liner
> Queen Elizabeth, New York,
> January 1946.

Friends/Friendship

Is there a dearer name than FRIEND? Think of it for me.

> **Abigail Adams**
> Letter to John Adams,
> October 25, 1782.

With this letter, I forward you a token of love and friendship.

> **Abigail Adams**
> Letter to Mercy Warren,
> December 30, 1812.

She was attempting to soothe the bitterness John Adams had toward Mrs. Warren, a close friend of the Adams family, but who had criticized him for having monarchistic tendencies. Mrs. Warren replied January 26, 1813, writing, "A token of love and friendship. What can be more acceptable to a mind of susceptibility?"

I have always believed that he [John Quincy Adams] both respected and loved me and did me justice in times when I needed a powerful friend.

Louisa Adams
Letter to brother-in-law Thomas Boylston Adams.

Friends are very important.

Barbara Bush
Former First Ladies Forum, Kennedy Center, Washington, D.C., March 9, 1998.

Anyone who knows my husband knows he enjoys people. He counts thousands, if not hundreds of thousands, of people among his friends. He likes spending time with people.

Hillary Rodham Clinton
White House press conference, remarking on criticism of White House fund-raising policy, March 10, 1997.

I am now alone and having laid our little son on the bed to sleep, employ a few moments in writing, having again perused your affectionate favor, and to return thanks to kind Providence for so tender a friend. Though I regret the loss of your society more than I can express, I am far happier in having you at distance with an assurance that you love me, than I should be in your society, doubting your affections.

Abigail Fillmore
Letter to Millard Fillmore, then serving his first term in the State Assembly, Albany, New York, January 17, 1830.

Think of me your dearest friend on earth.

Rachel Jackson
Letter to Andrew Jackson,
January 18, 1813.

Why is it so very rare in a man and woman to be simply intimate friends? Such a friendship is infinitely higher than what is usually called love, for in it there is a realization of each other's defects, and a proper appreciation of their good points without that fatal idealization which is so blind and, to me, so contemptable. . . . From my point of view a love which is worthy of the name should always have a beginning in the other. To have a man love you in any other way is no compliment.

Helen Taft
Writing in her diary in the
fall of 1880.

. . . I am fond only of what comes from the heart.

Martha Washington
Letter to Mary Otis Warren,
December 26, 1789.

Thereafter [her initial meeting with Woodrow Wilson] I never thought of him as the President of the United States, but as a real friend.

Edith Wilson
My Memoir, 1939.

Future

I don't have any idea what's going to happen. It's a constant surprise what I do and what happens to me.

Hillary Rodham Clinton
Having reached fifty, Mrs. Clinton
brushed aside questions about her
future during a White House press
conference, October 10, 1997.

. . . your future is almost as dependent on what you do in your periods of re-creating as in those of your creating.

Lou Henry Hoover
Radio speech to 4-H Clubs, NBC,
November 7, 1931.

. . . I believe that there is a future in anything that one is vitally interested in.

Lou Henry Hoover
Letter to Mary H. Helm,
February 6, 1942.

Gender

Desire and Sorrow were denounced upon our Sex; as a punishment for the transgression of Eve. I have sometimes thought that we are formed to experience more exquisite Sensations than is the Lot of your Sex. More tender and susceptable by Nature of those impressions which create happiness or misery, we Suffer and enjoy in a higher degree.

Abigail Adams
Letter to John Adams,
April 10, 1782.

I will never consent to have our sex considered in an inferior point of light. Let each planet shine in their own orbit. God and nature designed it so—if man is Lord, women is Lordess—that is what I contend for.

Abigail Adams
Letter to Elizabeth Shaw Peabody,
July 19, 1799.

I believe nature has assigned to each sex its particular duties and sphere of action, and to act well your part, there all the honor lies.

Abigail Adams
Letter to Francis Vanderkemp,
February 3, 1814.

. . . as it regards women the Adams family are one and all pecculiarly harsh and severe on their characters. There seems to exist no sympathy, no tenderness for the weakness of the sex . . .

> **Louisa Adams**
> Letter to Charles Frances Adams,
> youngest son, August 19, 1827.

When I see such Women as your Grandmother [Abigail Adams] go through years of exertion, of suffering, and of privation, with all the activity, judgment, skill and fortitude, which any man could display; I cannot believe there is any inferiority in the Sexes, as far as the mind and intellect are concerned, and man is aware of the fact . . . .

> **Louisa Adams**
> Letter to her son Charles Francis
> Adams, February 21, 1838.

There's no reason for us to be dividing women against women or men against women. This country needs people who want to reach beyond these boundaries and quit pointing fingers at one another.

> **Hillary Rodham Clinton**
> Comments, "This Morning," *CBS*,
> August 24, 1992.

Neither one [sex] can get along without the other—it is a cooperative thing.

> **Eleanor Roosevelt**
> White House press conference,
> February 19, 1945.

Goal

. . . our mission is not conquest, but understanding. Our weapons are not arms, but ideas. Our strategy and tactics are intellectual and scientific ingenuity. Our goal: Peaceful cooperation.

> **Claudia Lady Bird Johnson**
> Remarks at the Marshall Space Flight
> Center, Huntsville, Alabama,
> March 24, 1964.

I discovered I would find it difficult to just sit here and not do anything except entertain. For me, having a goal is important.

Nancy Reagan
Quoted, *Time*, January 14, 1985.

God

The race is not to the swift, nor the battle to the strong, but the God of Israel is he that giveth strength and power unto his people. Trust in him at all times, ye people pour out your hearts before him. God is a refuge for us.

Abigail Adams
Letter to John Adams, June 18, 1775.

[God is the] great power beyond us, that controls and guides us and all the affairs about us. . . . What we do know [about God], is that He has the strength and force and energy that we get to do things with. That He is the power that makes things happen in the world.

Lou Henry Hoover
Letter to her son, Herbert, aged
eleven, November 25, 1914.

Golden Rule

I pray you bear in mind that the golden rule of life is for each to attend to his own business, and let his neighbor's alone!

Julia Gardiner Tyler
An open letter, *Richmond Enquirer*,
January 28, 1853, to British women,
led by the Duchess of Sutherland,
who called on southern women to
end slavery.

Government

. . . Government of Good Laws well administered should carry with them the fairest prospect of happiness to a community, as well as to individuals.

Abigail Adams
Letter to John Adams, May 19, 1776.

. . . I think a balanced system of government, with three wheels interlocking, helping one another in orderly functioning, braking one another when one gets erratic, is better than any dictatorship, even a good one. . . .

Lou Henry Hoover
Letter to Allan Hoover,
May 17, 1933.

. . . imperceptibly we have come to recognize that government has a responsibility to defend the weak.

Eleanor Roosevelt
Comments on changing role of
government, White House,
March 2, 1935.

Ulysses S. Grant

He was a philosopher and a wise statesman as well as a great soldier.

Julia Dent Grant
*The Personal Memoirs of Julia Dent
Grant*, 1975.

Think of his kind thoughtfulness for me! He was always so forgiving, so charitable to my faults, and so generous to me.

Julia Dent Grant
On her husband's love and caring.
*The Personal Memoirs of Julia Dent
Grant*, 1975.

He makes a good general, but I should think, a very poor President.

Mary Lincoln
Letter to Elizabeth Blair Lee,
August 25, 1865.

Greatness

True greatness has its seat in the heart . . . it must be elevated by aspiring to great things and by daring to think yourself capable of them.

Abigail Adams
Letter to Royall Tyler, July 10, 1784.

It has been my experience that those who are truly great are the most simple people at heart, the most considerate and understanding, with a decided aversion of talking about themselves.

Grace Coolidge
Quoted by Ishbel Ross, *Grace Coolidge and Her Era*, 1962.

Grief

In grief, words are poor consolation—silence & agonizing tears, are all, that is left the sufferer.

Mary Lincoln
Letter to her sister Elizabeth Todd Edwards, March 19, 1877.

Guns

I hate guns.

Eleanor Roosevelt
Lecture, New Orleans, Louisiana,
March 6, 1937.

I confess I shudder every time I hear the sound of a gun.

Martha Washington
Letter to Elizabeth Ramsay,
December 30, 1775, referring to
guns fired in Boston.

Hair Style

I hate to break the myth, but you might as well know the truth. I have my hair done.

Barbara Bush
Debunking the popular misconception
that she does her own hair; press
conference, White House,
March 29, 1989.

Now I know your first choice today was Alice Walker—guess how I know?—known for *The Color Purple*. Instead you got me, known for the color of my hair!

Barbara Bush
Commencement address, Wellesley
College, Wellesley, Massachusetts,
June 1, 1990.

When the President called for sacrifice and asked everybody at the White House to take a 25 percent cut, I decided to take a 50 percent cut to do my part.

Hillary Rodham Clinton
Referring to her new haircut;
commencement address, University
of Pennsylvania, Philadelphia,
May 17, 1993.

One thing I can promise is that I will continue to change [it] to some extent.

Hillary Rodham Clinton
On the media fixation of how her
hair was done; *Parade Magazine*,
February 19, 1995.

. . . if you're the wife of the current sitting president, well, you just better make sure your hair is in place.

Hillary Rodham Clinton
Comments to graduating students,
University of Maryland, College Park,
Maryland, May 24, 1996.

I never wear a crown. It would mess up my hair.

Nancy Reagan
Jesting at the Alfred E. Smith
Memorial Dinner, New York,
October 1981.

Handsome

Mr. A. tells me his picture is likely to prove an excellent likeness at which I am much delighted as I think he never looked so well or so handsome as he does now.

Louisa Adams
Letter to her mother-in-law, Abigail
Adams, September 11, 1816. John
Quincy Adams was sitting for a
portrait by Charles Robert Leslie.

When I saw it, it was an admirable likeness; . . . He never looked handsomer or better than he does now.

Louisa Adams
Letter to her son, Charles Francis
Adams, January 26–28, 1838. Mrs.
Adams was telling her son that his
father was sitting for a bust by Shobal
Vail Clevenger.

One must not deem me partial if I say General Grant was the very nicest and handsomest man I ever saw . . .

Julia Dent Grant
*The Personal Memoirs of Julia Dent
Grant*, 1975.

Happiness

My heart is like a feather and my spirits are dancing.

> **Abigail Adams**
> Letter written April 1776, after she
> had received a packet of letters from
> her husband, John Adams.

. . . it is my wish and determination to be happy.

> **Lucretia Garfield**
> Diary, June 24, 1854.

It always seemed significant to me that Thomas Jefferson equated the pursuit of happiness with life and liberty itself. Men were born to be happy—just as they were born free.

> **Claudia Lady Bird Johnson**
> Remarks at the Congressional Prayer
> Breakfast, Washington, D.C.,
> February 1, 1967.

. . . it is one of my sources of happiness never to desire a knowledge of other people's business.

> **Dolley Madison**
> Letter to Benjamin Latrobe,
> September 12, 1809.

Being happy is a state of unconscious mind.

> **Edith Kermit Roosevelt**
> Letter to Ethel Roosevelt Derby,
> December 1, 1927.

When I was much younger I should, probably, have enjoyed gaieties of life as much as most my age, but I had long since placed all the prospects of my future worldly happiness in the still enjoyments of the fireplace at Mount Vernon.

> **Martha Washington**
> Letter to Mercy Otis Warren,
> December 26, 1789.

Harmony

Ugliness is so grim. A little beauty, something that is lovely, I think, can help create harmony which will lessen tensions.

Claudia Lady Bird Johnson
U.S. News & World Report,
February 22, 1965.

Health Care

I think people know there's a problem. I mean, people who have been denied health insurance because of pre-existing condition, who cannot change jobs because if they do they lose the insurance for their spouse and their child, people who are laid off and lose their benefits, . . . the hundred thousand Americans a month who lose their health insurance, people who have to wait in long lines to immunize their children . . .

Hillary Rodham Clinton
Comments to reporters following a
meeting with Senators at the U.S.
Capitol, February 4, 1993.

In the richest of all countries, there's a general sense of personal vulnerability and personal insecurity because the way our health care system has failed. . . . We don't have a system of health care, we have a patchwork, broken down system. . . . Unless you are willing to take on those who profit, you cannot provide the kind of universal immunization system this country needs to have.

Hillary Rodham Clinton
Speech, Health Care Forum,
Harrisburg, Pennsylvania,
February 11, 1993.

I hope . . . when our work is done, when the Congress had done what only the Congress can do to bring all of the disparate voices of America into these rooms to hammer out the choices that confront us, every American will receive a health security card guaranteeing a comprehensive package of benefits that can never be taken away under any circumstances.

Hillary Rodham Clinton
Testimony before the House of
Representative Ways and Means
Committee on a national health care
program, September 29, 1993.

It is time for . . . every American to stand up and say to the insurance industry: "Enough is enough. We want our health care system back."

Hillary Rodham Clinton
Address to the American Academy of
Pediatrics, Washington, D.C.,
November 1, 1993.

We have the finest doctors and hospitals in the world. We can beat any country when it comes to the quality of health care we have for those of us who are able to use it on a regular basis. But we do have probably the stupidest financing system in the world for health care. We spend money on paperwork, we spend money on bureaucracy, that we shouldn't have to spend.

Hillary Rodham Clinton
Speech, American Legion Annual
Conference, February 15, 1994.

You know, I have this old-fashioned idea that young people ought to help pay for old people and healthy people ought to help pay for sick people because at some point we're all going to be old.

Hillary Rodham Clinton
Modern Maturity,
February-March 1994.

When you're looking in the eyes of a sick child, you're not looking at a Democrat or a Republican, but an American who is in need of health care.

> **Hillary Rodham Clinton**
> Speech, National Education
> Association, New Orleans, Louisiana,
> July 3, 1994.

Americans want to have what members of Congress have: guaranteed health coverage.

> **Hillary Rodham Clinton**
> Speech at a rally in Portland, Oregon,
> July 22, 1994.

Providing health care to all our children is more than just a political challenge. It is a test of our faith in the future and of whether our rhetoric about family values will be translated into action on behalf of our children.

> **Hillary Rodham Clinton**
> "Thinking It Over," *The Washington Times*, May 22, 1997.

Hearing Problem

I'm one of every five people who suffers from tinnitus—commonly known as ringing-in-the-ears.

> **Rosalynn Carter**
> Remarks in advertisement for the
> Better Hearing Institute, 1997.

I know a lot of men who can't hear at all, but they are too vain to get hearing aids.

> **Hillary Rodham Clinton**
> Telling reporters that she was proud
> of her husband for agreeing to get
> hearing aids. White House,
> October 10, 1997.

Hecklers

I respect your right to think as you do. Now I'm asking you to be quiet while I finish what I have to say.

Claudia Lady Bird Johnson
Response to hecklers during
campaign speeches in 1964.

Hindsight

Hindsight is marvelous.

Nancy Reagan
Interview, *The New York Times,*
February 19, 1982.

History

I will be remembered.

Mary Lincoln
Letter to David Davis,
December 15, 1868.

For a while I thought history was something that bitter old men wrote. But then I realized history made Jack [Kennedy] what he was. . . . For Jack, history was full of heroes.

Jacqueline Kennedy
Quoted by Theodore R. White in *Life,*
December 6, 1963.

Home

I always had a fancy for a closet with a window which I could more peculiarly call my own.

Abigail Adams
Letter to John Adams, 1776.

What is home anyway? It is a place where mother runs a hotel for the accommodation of the rest of you? Or is it a place where you spend your leisure hours and a certain number of working hours cheerfully and happily together? The Girl Scout believes it is the latter place, and gives her best to making it so.

Lou Henry Hoover
Time, October 10, 1927.

Every woman wants a home of her own.

Claudia Lady Bird Johnson
Woman's Day, December 1967.

Running our home has always been a joy to me. I feel that this is what I was made for.

Jacqueline Kennedy
Boston Globe, January 15, 1961.

. . . my early home was truly at a boarding school.

Mary Lincoln
Letter to Elizabeth Keckley,
October 29, 1867.

I wish, dearest, you had just such a country home as this. I truly believe it is the happiest and most true life . . .

Dolley Madison
Letter to her sister, Anna Payne Cutts,
on living at Montpelier, Virginia,
July 5, 1820.

Here [Montpelier, Virginia] I find it most agreeable to stay at home, everything around me is so beautiful.

Dolley Madison
Letter to her niece, Mary Cutts,
July 30, 1826.

I love my home. It is important to us to have happy homes throughout the nation.

Patricia Pat Nixon
The New York Times,
December 11, 1957.

I assure you Mama my house outside and in is very elegant and quite becoming "a President's Lady."

Julia Gardiner Tyler
Letter to Juliana Gardiner, March 6,
1845, describing her new home at
Sherwood Forest, Virginia.

I cannot tell you, my dear friend, how much I enjoy home after having been deprived of one so long, for our dwelling in New York and Philadelphia was not home, only a sojourning.

Martha Washington
Letter to Mrs. Knox, 1797, upon
returning to Mount Vernon after
George Washington left the presidency.

Honesty

Mr. L [Lincoln] . . . is almost monomaniac on the subject of honesty . . .

Mary Lincoln
Letter to Abraham Wakeman,
September 23, 1864.

Honor

Honor, like the rainbow, flies the pursuer, and pursues the flier.

Dolley Madison
Statement written June 25, 1842.

Herbert Hoover

If you want to get the gloomiest view of any subject on earth, ask Bert [Herbert Hoover] about it.

Lou Henry Hoover
Literary Digest, September 8, 1917.

My husband will be back some day to do great things.

Lou Henry Hoover
Comment to White House housemaid Maggie Rogers upon leaving the White House.

Hope

What day is so dark that there is no ray of sunshine to penetrate the gloom?

Mary Lincoln
Letter to Emilie Todd Helm, November 23, 1856.

Housekeeping

Another change I made [in the White House staff] was the substitution of a housekeeper for a steward. I wanted a woman who could relieve me of supervision of such details as no man, expert steward though he might be, would ever recognize.

Helen Taft
Recollections of Full Years, 1914.

It takes just as much courage to stick to the housework until it is done as it does to go out and meet a bear.

Lou Henry Hoover
Speech, national convention of Girl Scout leaders, October 1927.

There are practical little things in housekeeping which no man really understands.

Eleanor Roosevelt
My Day, December 4, 1937.

I am again fairly settled down to the pleasant duties of an old-fashioned Virginia house-keeper, steady as a clock, busy as a bee, and cheerful as a cricket.

Martha Washington
Letter to Mrs. Knox, 1797, upon returning to Mount Vernon after George Washington retired from the presidency.

Housewife

I am perfectly satisfied to be known as a housewife.

Mamie Eisenhower
American Magazine, June 1948.

. . . I do not know how my reputation as a good housewife came about, as I always felt that in that respect I was not as good as I should be . . .

Julia Dent Grant
The Personal Memoirs of Julia Dent Grant, 1975.

Ambition in life: Not to be a housewife.

Jacqueline Kennedy
Writing in the class yearbook when she graduated from Miss Porter's School in Farmington, Connecticut, June 1947.

I guess I'd list myself as a housewife—with some experience in writing a column and in speaking—and that's all.

Eleanor Roosevelt
Press conference, March 1942.

Human Being

. . . I was a human being before I was the wife of a President . . .

Grace Coolidge
Comments in round robin letter to
her friends, 1928.

Human Nature

. . . whenever I meet a man I look first at his mouth, for I think it is the most important of all features; then I look at his ears—yes, you can learn a lot about a man's character from his ears—and then I study his eyes and the contour of his face. I am a great student of human nature. It is endless the things you can learn about human nature.

Florence Harding
Quoted, *The New York Times,*
April 25, 1923.

Everybody wants something.

Eleanor Roosevelt
Interview with Maureen Corr, 1960.

Human Rights

I don't think girls and women get as much attention on a regular basis as some of the well-publicized other instances of human rights concerns. I believe we have to emphasize as much as possible that the denial of education, the denial of basic health care, the denial of basic choices to girls is a human rights issue.

Hillary Rodham Clinton
Press interview, Colombo, Sri Lanka,
April 4, 1995.

If there is one message that echoes forth from this conference, it is that human rights are women's rights, and women's rights are human rights once and for all.

Hillary Rodham Clinton
Speech, United Nations Fourth
World Conference on Women,
Beijing, China, September 5, 1995.

It is not that you set the individual apart from society but that you recognize in any society that the individual must have rights that are guarded.

Eleanor Roosevelt
The New York Times,
February 4, 1947.

Where, after all, do universal rights begin? In small places, close to home—so close and so small that they cannot be seen on any map of the world. Yet they are the world of the individual person; the neighborhood he lives in; the school or college he attends; the factory, the farm or office where he works. Such are the places where every man, woman and child seeks equal justice, equal opportunity, equal dignity without discrimination. Unless these rights have meaning there, they have little meaning anywhere. Without concerned citizen action to uphold them close to home, we shall look in vain for progress in the larger world.

Eleanor Roosevelt
Remarks made at the presentation of
a booklet on human rights, *In Your
Hands,* to the United Nations
Commission on Human Rights,
United Nations, New York,
March 27, 1958.

Humble

Yes, faith and following the example of Christ can lead to transformation. But even after transformation we have to be humble, and we have to work hard to make sure that we don't elevate ourselves now that we have been transformed.

Hillary Rodham Clinton
Speech, National Prayer Breakfast,
Washington, D.C., February 6, 1997.

Humor

. . . when you know when to laugh and when to look upon things as too absurd to be taken seriously, the other person is ashamed to carry through even though he was serious about it.

Eleanor Roosevelt
Letter to Harry S. Truman,
May 14, 1945.

Good Lord! It's taken me years to get him to use the word *manure!*

Bess Truman
After her husband's speech to a
convention of farmers, when someone
asked, "Why on earth can't you get
Harry to use a more genteel word?"

Hunger

We cannot exist as a little island of well-being in a world where two-thirds of the people go to bed hungry every night.

Eleanor Roosevelt
Democratic Party dinner,
December 8, 1959.

Husband

I found his honor and reputation much dearer to me, than my own present pleasure and happiness . . .

Abigail Adams
Letter to Mercy Otis Warren,
January 1776.

I am ready and willing to follow my husband wherever he chooses.

Abigail Adams
Letter to John Adams,
April 26, 1797.

I am rather proud of the fact that after nearly a quarter of a century of marriage, my husband feels free to make his decisions and act upon them without consulting me or giving me advance information concerning them.

Grace Coolidge
Autobiographical article, *American Magazine*, August 1929.

I have scant patience with the man of whom his wife says, "He never gave me a cross word in his life." It seems to me he must be a feckless creature. If a man amounts to much in this world, he must encounter many and varied annoyances whose number mounts as his effectiveness increases. Inevitably comes a point beyond which human endurance breaks down, and an explosion is bound to follow.

Grace Coolidge
On the idiosyncrasies of husbands.

Your husband is the boss—and don't forget it.

Mamie Eisenhower
"If I Were a Bride Today," *True Confessions*, November 1954.

What in this world can compensate for the sympathy and confidence of a mother and a sister—nothing but the tie that binds us to a good husband. Such are ours and we ought to be satisfied.

Dolley Madison
Letter to Anna Cutts, June 3, 1808.

A wife always finds her husband out sooner or later!

Ellen Axson Wilson
Letter to Woodrow Wilson,
April 3, 1892.

Saddam Hussein

I detest him. Is that strong enough? . . . I'd like to see him hung, if he were found guilty [of war crimes].

Barbara Bush
Comments to reporters at a White House lunch, April 15, 1991.

Ideas

I see some of my ideas put into practice. I'm not sure Lyndon remembers where he got them.

Claudia Lady Bird Johnson
Time, November 29, 1963.

Illiteracy

I have a very simple aim—to wipe out illiteracy. I am going to really encourage reading programs . . .

Barbara Bush
Interview, *The New York Times*,
February 22, 1981.

The climate is right for a major attack on illiteracy, one national problem for which the cure is known.

Barbara Bush
"Our Reading Problem," Op-ed article she wrote for *The Washington Post*, August 2, 1984.

... I urge you to help the young . . . out there today . . . enslaved by ignorance, to learn their ABCs . . .

Barbara Bush
Commencement speech, Bennett College, Greensboro, North Carolina, May 14, 1989.

Illness

I am feeling very miserable, headache most of the time . . .

Ida McKinley
Diary, April 15, 1901. Mrs. McKinley suffered from various illnesses for many years.

I think any illness brings a family closer together. It brings things into focus and should reshuffle your priorities.

Nancy Reagan
Newsweek, October 2, 1995.

Imagination

I think imagination is one of the greatest blessings of life . . .

Edith Roosevelt
Letter to Theodore Roosevelt, June 8, 1886.

Immigration

Lucy Hayes

For the most part, in the first century after the Declaration of Independence immigrants were from the most civilized nations of Europe, and were seeking liberty and land for homes. Now, however, an increasing number of them come or are brought from the less enlightened European nations and from heathen countries, seeking simply better wages, and caring little or nothing for land or homes. They are sadly lacking in education and religion, and are by no means well fitted for the citizenship of a republic.

Lucy Hayes
Diary, April 2, 1881.

Immortality

I do believe in immortality, but I haven't been able to decide exactly what form it might take. There are so many possibilities. For example, there is a question in my mind whether we will appear physically as we appear now. It seems unnecessary to try to decide the exact form that immortality will take. We won't be able to change it and we must accept it. And we must meet it with courage and do our best.

Eleanor Roosevelt
Interview in Paris, France,
September 10, 1951.

Impeachment

I knew he'd be acquitted; I knew it . . .

Eliza Johnson
Remarks to White House aide
William Henry Crook, who brought
her word that her husband Andrew
Johnson had escaped impeachment,
May 26, 1868.

Impressions

. . . men see things as they wish to see them.

Edith Wilson
My Memoir, 1939.

Independence

I want to be who I want to be and I don't want to be told I can or can not do something that is natural and part of my life.

Hillary Rodham Clinton
Interview, *The New York Times*,
May 7, 1994.

I have an independence streak. You know, it is kind of hard to tell an independent woman what to do.

Betty Ford
Interview with Leslie Stahl, *60 Minutes* CBS-TV, October 12, 1997.

I wanted to be independent. I was beginning to realize that something within me craved to be an individual.

Eleanor Roosevelt
On leaving her mother-in-law's
house in Hyde Park and setting up
housekeeping with her husband,
who had been elected to the New
York State Senate in Albany, 1911.
This Is My Story, 1937.

I thought that a woman should be independent and not regard matrimony as the only thing to be desired in life.

> **Helen Taft**
> Diary of Helen Herron, Papers of
> William Howard Taft,
> Library of Congress.

I very sincearly [sic] wish you would exert yourself so as to keep all your matters in order yourself without depending upon others as that is the only way to be happy—to have all your business in your own hands without trusting to others . . . look upon this advice in the friendly way it is meant, as I wish you to be as independent as your circumstances will admit and to be so, is to exert yourself in the management of your estate. If you do not no one else will. A dependence is, I think, a wrached [wretched] state and you will have enough if you will manage it right.

> **Martha Washington**
> Letter to Fanny Bassett Washington,
> September 15, 1794.

Individuality

One man can make a difference and every man should try.

> **Jacqueline Kennedy Onassis**
> Mrs. Onassis wrote this sentence on
> a card to accompany an exhibit that
> traveled around the country when
> the John F. Kennedy Library in
> Boston was first opened.

Infidelity

You have to understand, my husband loved people. All people. And half of the people in the world were women. You don't think I could have kept my husband away from half the people? [Alluding to her husband's infidelities.]

> **Claudia Lady Bird Johnson**
> *People*, February 2, 1987.

Inferiority

The sense of inferiority which by nature and by law we are compelled to feel and to which we must submit, is worn by us with as much satisfaction as the badge of slavery generally, and we love to be flattered out of our sense of our degradation.

Louisa Adams
Letter to John Quincy Adams,
August 1822.

Influence

When you've been married 47 years, if you don't have any influence, then I really think you're in deep trouble.

Barbara Bush
Los Angeles Times, May 31, 1992.

The President of the United States cares what I think. I have influence and I'm aware of it.

Rosalynn Carter
Speech, New York Women in
Communications Inc., New York,
March 26, 1997.

I don't think that there is any doubt that the First Ladies have some influence on their husbands, because they are close to them, they talk with them all the time, they have the presidents' ear. I don't think there is any doubt about it.

Rosalynn Carter
Former First Ladies Forum, Kennedy
Center, Washington, D.C.,
March 9, 1998.

Injustice

The more I bear the more is expected of me, and I sink the efforts I make to answer such expectations. Thus sickness passes for ill temper and suffering for unwillingness and I am decried an incumberance unless I am required for any special purpose for a show or for some political maneouvre and if I wish for a trifle of any Kind any favour is required at my hands a deaf ear is turned to my request. Arrangements are made and if I object I am informed it is too late and it is all a misunderstanding.

Louisa Adams
Letter to Mary Hellen Adams,
August 19, 1827.

Intimidate

I am not apt to be intimidated you know.

Abigail Adams
Letter to John Adams,
September 20, 1777.

Investments

The heart and soul of the American economy . . . is risk-taking and investing in the future.

Hillary Rodham Clinton
News conference called to discuss
her stock purchases, Washington, D.C.,
April 22, 1994.

Isolation

The habit of living almost entirely alone has a tendency to render us savages. However sentimental you think me, I will say that isolation is an evil . . . and one likely to be productive of insanity in a weak woman.

Louisa Adams
Letter to her son Charles Francis
Adams, complaining of the loneliness
of living in the White House, 1828.

Andrew Jackson

Of all the presidents of the United States, there are only a few, I believe, whose image remains strongly with us today. Men whom we can visualize as having once been flesh and blood and not vague shadows on the pages of history. For me, Andrew Jackson was one of these men.

Claudia Lady Bird Johnson
Remarks at The Hermitage on the
first-day-issue stamp ceremony com-
memorating 200th anniversary of
Andrew Jackson's birth; Nashville,
Tennessee, March 15, 1967.

Of some men you will hear it said that they were either for or against something. General Jackson was always for something. Of course, in being for one thing he always must be against some other thing, its opposite or antithesis. But the "being for" was what filled his soul. The being against was secondary or incidental—necessary and unavoidable, as a rule.

Sarah Childress Polk
Quoted by Augustus C. Buell in
History of Andrew Jackson, 1904.

Thomas Jefferson

. . . Mr. Jefferson. He is one of the choice ones of the earth.

Abigail Adams
Letter to Mary Smith Cranch,
May 8, 1785.

Jelly Beans

I like them [jelly beans], but not as much as my husband.

Nancy Reagan
To third graders at Chicago's Latin
School, May 14, 1982.

Jobs

I really believe it's good for you to get a new subject about every ten years. Unless you have a burning desire to be a doctor or president of a bank, probably it's a good thing to shift jobs, meet new people, take on new projects.

Barbara Bush
Interview, *The Washington Post*,
June 5, 1988.

Andrew Johnson

. . . that miserable inebriate Johnson . . .

Mary Lincoln
Letter to Sally Orne,
March 15, 1866.

Claudia Lady Bird Johnson

I have to confess that Lady Bird is [role model as First Lady]—maybe because she's a fellow Texan—but I think it is because she's an enormous lady. But she said, you know, that the White House is a bully pulpit and you ought to take advantage of it. And we tried to do something every day that would help somebody in some way in our country.

> **Barbara Bush**
> Former First Ladies Forum,
> Kennedy Center, Washington, D.C.,
> March 9, 1998.

I don't need to tell you here what I think of her [Mrs. Johnson] qualities—her extraordinary grace of character—her willingness to assume every burden—She assumed so many for me and I love her very much . . .

> **Jacqueline Kennedy**
> Letter to President Lyndon B.
> Johnson, November 26, 1963,
> thanking him and Mrs. Johnson for
> their comfort following the death of
> John F. Kennedy.

Lyndon B. Johnson

He's a good man in a tight spot.

> **Claudia Lady Bird Johnson**
> Commenting on her husband's conduct immediately after the assassination of President Kennedy. From her taped White House diary covering events of November 22–24, 1963.

I knew I had something remarkable, but I didn't know quite what.

> **Claudia Lady Bird Johnson**
> Recalling that Lyndon B. Johnson proposed to her on their first date. Ten weeks later they were married. *Time*, November 29, 1963.

I thought that you looked strong, firm and like a reliable guy . . .

Claudia Lady Bird Johnson
Telephone conversation with
President Lyndon B. Johnson, March
7, 1964, offering her critique of his
press conference that day.

He always expected more of you than you're really mentally or
physically capable of putting out. Somehow that makes you try a
little bit harder, and makes you produce a little more. It is really a
very good fertilizer for growth; it's also very tiring.

Claudia Lady Bird Johnson
Ruth Montgomery, *Mrs. LBJ*, 1964.

Journalism

Journalism, will naturally lead to a love for politics, & I think, that is
anything, but desirable in a young man.

Mary Lincoln
Letter to Edward Lewis Baker, Jr.,
April 11, 1877.

Joy

Joy is importantly different from mere pleasure. Joy has in it the real
recognition of the contrasts and depths and problems of life. Joy is an
act of courage because it can carry you through anxieties and sorrow.

Claudia Lady Bird Johnson
Remarks at the Congressional Prayer
Breakfast, Washington, D.C.,
February 1, 1967.

Justice

. . . remember truth and justice have two ears.

Abigail Adams
Letter to Elizabeth Shaw Peabody,
January 13, 1814.

Justice and Mercy should go together.

Lucy Hayes
On healing the nation's wounds from the Civil War; letter to Rutherford B. Hayes, April 17, 1865.

Kennedy Family

It was a marvelous weekend. How can I explain these people? They were like carbonated water, and other families might be flat.

Jacqueline Kennedy
After meeting the Kennedy family in the summer of 1952 at Hyannis Port, Massachusetts

Jacqueline Kennedy

I do want to express my admiration for all the ways you found to help your husband in that great endeavor of his life. . . . you certainly made a great contribution. . . . It is going to be very nice to have you as First Lady.

Claudia Lady Bird Johnson
Letter to Jacqueline Kennedy, November 10, 1960. Mrs. Johnson complimented Mrs. Kennedy for campaigning for her husband, John F. Kennedy, despite her pregnancy.

We were distant. But that suited both of us.

Claudia Lady Bird Johnson
The Washington Post, March 23, 1995.

John F. Kennedy

John F. Kennedy believed strongly that one's aim should not be the most comfortable life possible—but that we should all do something to right the wrongs we see—and not just complain about them. We owe that to our country, and our country will suffer if we don't serve her. He believed that one person can make a difference—and that every person should try.

> **Jacqueline Kennedy Onassis**
> Statement on the plans for the
> John F. Kennedy Library.

I should have known that it was asking too much to dream that I might have grown old with him. . . . So now he is a legend when he would have preferred to be a man.

> **Jacqueline Kennedy**
> Describing her feelings since the
> assassination of her husband, written
> for *Look* magazine "JFK Memorial
> Issue," November 17, 1964.

He lived at such a pace because he wished to know it all.

> **Jacqueline Kennedy**
> Quoted, Arthur M. Schlesinger, Jr.,
> *A Thousand Days*, 1965.

Kitchens

I never go into the kitchens.

> **Lou Henry Hoover**
> When the new First Lady, Eleanor
> Roosevelt, asked Mrs. Hoover to
> show her the White House kitchen.

Ladies

I meet with more accomplishment among the ladies of Virginia than is usually met with those of New York State. They have generally more talent and finer manners, more self-possession, which is owing I think to their priding themselves so much on their native state, "The Old Dominion"—the home or birthplace of so many Presidents.

Julia Gardiner Tyler
Letter to her sister Margaret
Gardiner, April 10, 1845.

Languages

I found it very frustrating to have only one language. I only speak English and that I think was a big drawback. It is one of the things that is a very sizeable asset to be able to converse in two or three languages.

Claudia Lady Bird Johnson
Oral history interview, Lyndon Baines
Johnson Library, October 10, 1990.

. . . every child throughout the world should learn the language of his own country and one agreed language, which would be the same all over the world.

Eleanor Roosevelt
Suggesting a United Nations move
for compulsory teaching of one inter-
nationally understood language in
schools throughout the world;
London, January 26, 1946.

I'm not going back without knowing basic Russian—at least the rudiments. It is awful to be where you can't understand one word.

Eleanor Roosevelt
Press interview, Washington, D.C.,
October 10, 1957.

Laughter

One of the reasons I made the most important decision of my life, to marry George Bush, is because he made me laugh. It's true, sometimes we laugh through our tears, but that shared laughter has been one of our strongest bonds.

Barbara Bush
Commencement address, Wellesley
College, Wellesley, Massachusetts,
June 1, 1990.

We grow up when we have our first good laugh—at ourselves.

Eleanor Roosevelt
Quoted, Gerald Gardner, *All the
Presidents' Wits*, 1986.

Fortunately, we are a family that laughs.

Helen Taft
Recollections of Full Years, 1914.

Laws

Can any government be free which is not administered by general stated laws?

Abigail Adams
Letter to John Adams,
November 27, 1775.

Leadership

If we do not lay ourselves in the service of mankind whom should we serve?

Abigail Adams
Letter to John Thaxter,
September 29, 1778.

We don't lead out of perfection, but out of our comprehension of God's vision.

Hillary Rodham Clinton
Comments at an interdenominational
faith meeting, New York,
July 11, 1992.

So I say: Don't hold back. Don't be shy. Step forward in every way you can to plan boldly, to speak clearly, to offer the leadership which the world needs.

Claudia Lady Bird Johnson
Speech, National Convention of
American Home Economics
Association, Detroit, June 24, 1964.

Spiritual leadership should remain spiritual leadership and the temporal power should not become too important in any church.

Eleanor Roosevelt
Letter to Cardinal Francis Spellman,
July 23, 1949.

I believe it is a great mistake not to stand up for people, even when you differ with them, if you feel that they are trying to do things that will help our country.

Eleanor Roosevelt
The Nation, June 7, 1952.

Learning

Youth is the proper season for observation and attention—a mind unencumbered with cares may seek instruction and draw improvement from all the objects which surround it. The earlier in life you accustome yourself to consider objects with attention, the easier will your progress be, and more sure and successful your enterprises. What a Harvest of true knowledge and learning may you gather from the numberless varied Scenes through which you pass if you are not wanting in your own assiduity and endeavours.

Abigail Adams
Letter to John Quincy Adams,
January 21, 1781.

We learned by doing and they [young people] will learn by doing, too.

Eleanor Roosevelt
Address at White House Conference
on Children in a Democracy,
January 20, 1940.

Legacy

I hope I'm remembered for the drug program and the help to children.

Nancy Reagan
Interview, *The Associated Press*,
January 14, 1989.

Legal Services

I never thought that being for legal service, which I have been for 22 years, is "liberal." Legal services is the bedrock issue for equal justice and an absolute imperative to have available. I don't think that is liberal or conservative. I think that's how you make a justice system work. I view it as a very pragmatic response to real people's needs.

Hillary Rodham Clinton
Interview, *The Washington Post*,
August 1, 1992.

Legs

. . . I think that a gentleman has no business to concern himself about the Legs of a lady . . .

Abigail Adams
Letter to John Adams, May 9, 1764.

Leisure

The leisure class is one in which individuals have sufficient economic security and sufficient leisure to find opportunity for a variety of satisfactions in life.

Eleanor Roosevelt
White House press conference,
February 10, 1936.

Letters/Letter Writing

Five weeks have passed and not one line have I received. I had rather give a dollar for a letter by post, tho the consequence should be that I Eat but one meal a day for these three weeks to come.

Abigail Adams
Letter to John Adams,
September 17, 1774.

My pen is always freer than my tongue. I have wrote many things to you that I supposed I never could have talk'd.

Abigail Adams
Letter to John Adams,
October 22, 1775.

. . . your Letters never fail to give me pleasure, be the subject what it will . . .

Abigail Adams
Letter to John Adams,
July 14, 1776.

When ever I receive a Letter from you it seems to give new Springs to my nerves, and a brisker circulation to my Blood.

Abigail Adams
Letter to Mary Cranch,
July 15, 1776.

There are particular times when I feel such uneasiness, such a restlessness, as neither company, Books, family Cares or other thing will remove, my Pen is my only pleasure and writing to you the composure of my mind.

Abigail Adams
Letter to John Adams,
September 23, 1776.

Let me entreat you to write me more letters. . . . They are my food by day and my rest by night.

Abigail Adams
Letter to John Adams,
February 1779.

[Her son John Quincy] has forgotten to use his pen.

Abigail Adams
Letter to John Adams, November 11,
1783.

I will not deny that there may be a little vanity in the hope of being honourd with a line from you.

Abigail Adams
Letter to Thomas Jefferson,
June 7, 1785.

My letters to you are first thoughts, without corrections.

Abigail Adams
Letter to Mary Cranch,
May 26, 1798.

If someone buys a card and takes time to write, the least I can do is to thank them.

Mamie Eisenhower
McCall's, October 1976.

Write me all the news. You cannot imagine how any little circumstances concerning my friends interests me when absent so far from them.

> **Abigail Fillmore**
> Letter to Maria Fuller,
> August 27, 1826.

I have just received one of the most affectionate letters you have ever written. I was alone and gave vent to my feelings, but I shed no tears of grief. . . . The perusal of your letter added new energies to my soul and tenderness (if possible) to my heart.

> **Abigail Fillmore**
> Letter to Millard Fillmore,
> January 16, 1830.

Take pains my dear little boy that every letter we receive from you is written better than the last one.

> **Abigail Fillmore**
> Letter to her son, Millard, attending a
> boarding school, January 19, 1838.

You must write often William to someone of the family, for I shall always be uneasy unless you do, . . .

> **Anna Harrison**
> Letter to her son William,
> May 8, 1819.

I Could write you all Day Long but such a Pen I feare you never Can read it . . .

> **Rachel Jackson**
> Letter to Andrew Jackson during a
> military campaign in 1813.

Oh, that I had the pen of a ready writer . . .

> **Rachel Jackson**
> Letter to Mrs. Kingsley, July 23, 1821.

And, if you think your letters-to-the-editor columns bring a variety of opinions, I invite you to come read mine. But, let me point out, all you have to do is to print them. I have to answer them.

Claudia Lady Bird Johnson
Address at luncheon of the annual convention of the Associated Press Managing Editors Association, Washington, D.C., October 1, 1965.

This writing paper was especially designed for writing heads of state—do you think it is good enough?

Jacqueline Kennedy
Note to Oleg Cassini, 1961.

Some letters really do help— . . .

Jacqueline Kennedy
On the death of her son Patrick; letter to Arthur M. Schlesinger, Jr., August 26. 1963.

How much I wish instead of writing, we were together this evening.

Mary Lincoln
Letter to Abraham Lincoln, May 1848.

. . . there is a great deal in getting out of the habit of letter writing, once I was very fond of it, nothing pleases me now better than receiving a letter from an absent friend . . .

Mary Lincoln
Letter to Emilie Todd Helm, November 23, 1856.

I have waited in vain to hear from you, yet as you are not given to letter writing, will be charitable enough to impute your silence, to the right cause.

Mary Lincoln
Letter to Abraham Lincoln, November 2, 1862.

I am sorry to trouble you, but you know that a woman's letter is incomplete without a postscript.

> **Mary Lincoln**
> Comments to a reporter of the
> *Boston Journal* who waited for her to
> write a note he was to mail to her
> husband. Mrs. Lincoln was at Mount
> Washington recuperating from an
> accident, August 1863.

Please burn this, for I have written in the bitterness of my sad heart.

> **Mary Lincoln**
> Letter to Mary Jane Welles,
> December 29, 1865.

My ink is like myself and my spirits failing, so I write you to-day with a pencil.

> **Mary Lincoln**
> Letter to Elizabeth Keckley,
> October 6, 1867.

It is now past nine o'clock, and I cease to write, only to dream of thee.

> **Dolley Madison**
> Letter to James Madison,
> October 30, 1805.

There has been a spell upon my fingers for a long time, dearest niece, and even now there rests one on my eyes; still I would commune with you, whom I love so much, and tell you that your letters are received, and my spirits rising as I peruse them . . .

> **Dolley Madison**
> Letter to Mary Cutts,
> December 2, 1834.

I'm anxious to hear from you, not political prospects only but your good health.

> **Sarah Childress Polk**
> Letter to James K. Polk,
> June 15, 1839.

I do hope when you receive this note you will not say to yourself that your wife is as annoying as the office-seekers, persecuting you wherever you go by compelling you to open and read a little budget of nonsense of my own sad complaints that I am separated from you. . . . How often do you intend to write me?

Sarah Childress Polk
Letter to James K. Polk,
August 19, 1848.

I know when I am in the White House I shall look forward eagerly to the morning's mail, just as I have ever since I was a little girl.

Eleanor Roosevelt
Radio talk, *NBC*, February 17, 1933.

. . . whatever happens to us in our lives, we find questions constantly recurring that we would gladly discuss with some friend. Yet it is hard to find just the friend we should like to talk to. Often it is easier to write to someone whom we do not expect ever to see.

Eleanor Roosevelt
"I Want You to Write to Me,"
Woman's Home Companion,
August 1933.

I am typing this because I know my husband always preferred to have things typed so he could read them more quickly and my handwriting is anything but legible.

Eleanor Roosevelt
Letter to President Harry S. Truman
May 14, 1945.

Write to your Representative in Congress. Writing to me is of very little use!

Eleanor Roosevelt
My Day, April 30, 1946. Exhorting
her readers to support price control
until the country regains full production after the end of World War II.

I could continue with my pen without fatigue, but it is a late hour, . . .

Julia Gardiner Tyler
Letter to her mother, Juliana
Gardiner, May 7, 1861.

I wrote to you several times in hopes that would put you in mind of me, but I find it has not had its intended affect and I am really very uneasy at not hearing from you and have made all the excuses for you that I can think of, but it will not doe much longer, if I doe [sic] not get a letter by this night's post, I shall think myself quite forgot by all my Friends. The distance is long yet the post comes regularly every week.

Martha Washington
Letter to her sister Nancy Bassett,
January 31, 1776.

. . . if you do not write to me—I will not write to you again or till I get letters from you.

Martha Washington
Letter to her son John Parke and
daughter-in-law Eleanor Custis,
March 17, 1778.

. . . by some neglect of the post master my letters does not come regularly to hand.

Martha Washington
Letter to her brother Bartholomew
Dandridge, November 1778.

Your very friendly letter of last month has afforded me much more satisfaction than all the formal compliments and empty ceremonies of mere etiquette could possibly have done.

Martha Washington
Letter to Mary Otis Warren,
December 26, 1789, expressing her
feelings about becoming First Lady
following George Washington's inauguration as the first American president in New York on April 30, 1789.

Will you forgive a pencil tonight? For I am in bed where I cannot use ink without endangering some very lovely linen things in the way of sheets and pillow cases— . . .

Edith Wilson
Letter to Woodrow Wilson,
August 5, 1915.

. . . coupled with the natural diffuseness of womanhood, is that we really don't know how to write a short letter; we wander along as though time were no more, and are only beginning to get fairly warmed up and into our subject, such as it is, when we reach the third sheet.

Ellen Axson Wilson
Letter to Woodrow Wilson,
September 1, 1883.

How do you expect me to keep my head, you dear thing, when you send me such letters as you have done recently—when you lavish upon me such delicious praise? Surely there was never such a lover before, and even after all these years it seems almost too good to be true that you are my lover. All I can say in return is that I love you as you deserve to be loved,—as much as you can possibly want to be loved.

Ellen Axson Wilson
Letter to Woodrow Wilson,
August 27, 1902.

Liberal

I'm a liberal when it comes to human rights, the poor, so's George Bush . . . but liberal and conservative doesn't mean much to me anymore. Does that mean we care about people and are interested and want to help? And if that makes you a liberal, so be it.

Barbara Bush
Interview with Jim Miklaszewski,
NBC, November 15, 1989.

Liberty

. . . for sure it were better never to have known the blessings of Liberty than to have enjoyed it, and then to have it ravished from us.

Abigail Adams
Letter to Isaac Smith, Jr.,
April 20, 1771.

It is not better to die the last of British freemen than live the first of British slaves?

Abigail Adams
Letter to Mercy Otis Warren,
February 2, 1776.

We do not move forward by curtailing people's liberty because we are afraid of what they may do or say. We move forward by assuring to all people protection in the basic liberties under a democratic form of government, and then making sure that our government serves the real needs of the people.

Eleanor Roosevelt
"Fear Is the Enemy," *The Nation*,
February 10, 1940.

Library

. . . a library is dead if not used.

Jacqueline Kennedy
Letter to Arthur M. Schlesinger, Jr.,
February 21, 1963.

Lies

There used to be this old saying that the lie can be halfway around the world before the truth gets its boots on. Well, today, the lie can be twice around the world before the truth gets out of bed to find its boots.

Hillary Rodham Clinton
Commenting on how fast false news, through the twenty-four-hour media, like the Internet, can instantaneously be flashed around the world. Press conference, White House, February 11, 1998.

I know I can't lie.

Betty Ford
Helen Thomas, *Dateline: White House*, 1975.

Life

Tho I sometimes like to mix in the gay world, . . . I have much reason to be grateful to my parents that my early education gave me not a habitual taste for what is termed fashionable life.

Abigail Adams
Letter to Mary Cranch, January 26, 1786.

What is life or its enjoyments without . . . mental exertions—a mere vapor indeed.

Abigail Adams
Letter to Lucy Cranch, April 25, 1787.

Who of us pass through the world with our path strewed with flowers, without encountering the thorns? In what ever state we are we shall find a mixture of good and evil, and we must learn to receive these vicissitudes of life, so as not to be unduly exalted by one, or depressed by the other.

Abigail Adams
Letter to Mary Cranch, October 31, 1799.

My life has been a life of changes . . .

Louisa Adams
Letter to John Quincy Adams

I believe life is right now.

Barbara Bush
The Washington Post,
February 1, 1989.

At the end of your life, you will never regret not having passed one more test, not winning one more verdict, or not closing one more deal. You will regret time not spent with a husband, a friend, a child, or a parent.

Barbara Bush
Commencement address, Wellesley College, Wellesley, Massachusetts, June 1, 1990.

I have not had my life yet. It is all before me . . .

Frances Cleveland
Upon leaving the White House, quoted, *The New York Times,* March 4, 1889.

. . . I think everyone should really think about how to prepare children once they get to be a certain age for the realities of life.

Hillary Rodham Clinton
Time, June 3, 1996.

. . . both Jerry [Ford] and I believe that if you can save the life of one person—just one—then you have accomplished your mission in life.

Betty Ford
McCall's, February 1975.

. . . I believe life is pretty well planned for you, and what will be, will be . . .

Betty Ford
McCall's, February 1975.

I believe in living day to day—or hour to hour— . . .

Betty Ford
Quoted by Helen Thomas, *Dateline: White House*, 1975.

I enjoy the moment for the moment, take everything out of what I'm doing one step at a time, and when it's gone I will have lived that time to the fullest.

Betty Ford
Quoted by Barbara Goldsmith, *Parade*, May 1, 1983.

It seems to be the more you know about life, the more you get out of it.

Lou Henry Hoover
View expressed to reporters covering the annual convention of the Girl Scouts of America, Indianapolis, October 1, 1930.

If you can achieve the precious balance between woman's domestic and civic life, you can do more for zest and sanity in our society than by any other achievement.

Claudia Lady Bird Johnson
Speech, Radcliffe College, Cambridge, Massachusetts, June 9, 1964.

I always live for the present.

Patricia Pat Nixon
Ladies' Home Journal, November 1960.

I never had time to think about . . . who I admired, or to have ideas. I never had time to dream about being anyone else. I had to work. My parents died when I was a teen-ager. . . . I've never had it easy.

Patricia Pat Nixon
Interview with Gloria Steinem, *New York*, October 29, 1968.

Patricia Pat Nixon

The fire of life sinks for one generation, but its flames leap high for another.

Edith Kermit Roosevelt
Cleared for Strange Ports, 1927.

. . . the only thing that really matters is your inner conviction that at least you are attempting to do what you consider your job, and that outside of that nothing really counts.

Eleanor Roosevelt
White House press conference,
February 21, 1936.

The things that happen in life are not as important as what they do to people, . . . I don't think most people lead happy lives.

Eleanor Roosevelt
Statement at a literary reception,
New York, February 24, 1937.

I could not, at any age, be content to take my place in a corner by the fireside and simply look on. Life was meant to be lived. Curiosity must be kept alive. The fatal thing is the rejection. One must never, for whatever reason, turn his back on life.

Eleanor Roosevelt
New York Herald Tribune,
October 11, 1961.

You can never really live anyone else's life, not even your child's. The influence you exert is through your own life, and what you've become yourself.

Eleanor Roosevelt
Quoted by Julia Gilden and Mark
Riedman, *Woman to Woman*, 1994.

Ah dearest love, what a difference between the old and the new,— how sweet was that—how infinitely sweeter this!

Ellen Axson Wilson
Observations after making a senti-
mental journey to the South; letter to
Woodrow Wilson, April 3, 1892.

Abraham Lincoln

. . . with trembling anxiety I had been permitted to watch over and minister to my idolized husband, through an illness and receiving his loving farewell words in return, I could have thanked him for his life-long—almost; devotion to me & mine, and I could have asked for-giveness, for any inadvertant moment of pain, I may have caused him . . .

> **Mary Lincoln**
> Letter to Charles Sumner,
> April 10, 1866.

. . . lover—husband—father—all.

> **Mary Lincoln**
> Describing her husband in a letter to
> Sally Orne, December 12, 1869.

Liquor

It's really kind of funny to me to see people kind of squirm because we don't serve liquor in the White House.

> **Rosalynn Carter**
> Interview, *The New York Times*
> March 15, 1977.

Literacy

I chose literacy because I honestly believe that if more people could read, write, and comprehend, we would be that much closer to solv-ing so many of the problems plaguing our society.

> **Barbara Bush**
> Commencement address, Wellesley
> College, Wellesley, Massachusetts,
> June 1, 1990.

I really feel that if everybody could read, write and comprehend, we would have less crime, less teenage pregnancies, all the things that you and I worry about.

Barbara Bush
Former First Ladies Forum, Kennedy
Center, Washington, D.C.,
March 9, 1998.

Locomotive

It is not difficult to imagine it some monster of an animal, and I must confess I almost felt inclined "to run."

Lucretia Garfield
Reaction to seeing her first railroad
locomotive. Diary,
September 6, 1851.

Loneliness

Sunday seems a more Lonesome Day to me than any other when you are absent.

Abigail Adams
Letter to John Adams,
September 13, 1767.

I want a companion at Nights, many of them are wakefull and Lonesome, . . . I wish the day past, yet dread its arrival.

Abigail Adams
Letter to John Adams,
June 23, 1777.

How lonely are my days? How solitary are my Nights?

Abigail Adams
Letter to John Adams,
December 27, 1778.

You have scarcely been out of my mind during the day.

Abigail Fillmore
Letter to Millard Fillmore,
January 17, 1829.

Mr. Pierce has just left here to be gone all the week. I hardly know what to do without him . . .

Jane Pierce
Letter to Mary Aiken, July 1839.

Love

Ever remember with the Tenderest Sentiments her who knows no earthly happiness equal to that of being tenderly loved by her dearest Friend.

Abigail Adams
Letter to John Adams,
April 17, 1777.

Words cannot convey to you the tenderness of my affection.

Abigail Adams
Letter to John Adams,
August 22, 1777.

If I were to tell you all the tenderness of my heart, I should do nothing but write to you.

Abigail Adams
Letter to John Adams,
February 1779.

The falling out of Lovers is the renewal of Love.

Abigail Adams
Letter to John Adams,
November 13, 1780.

. . . the more I know you the more I admire, esteem and love you, and the greater is my inclination to do everything in my power to promote your happiness and welfare.

Louisa Adams
Letter to John Quincy Adams,
May 26, 1797.

If lovers' quarrels are a renewal of love, they also leave a sting behind which apparently heal'd reopens on every trivial occasion . . .

Louisa Adams
Record of a Life, My Story,
July 23, 1825.

Oh guide me, guide me that I may prove worthy of one so good and true, if he may be mine.

Lucretia Garfield
Diary, August 27, 1855.

What a new world I am living in. All my life before has been in a mist—a cloud . . . O how beautiful to live in such a world of light and love. . . .

Lucretia Garfield
Letter to James A. Garfield,
September 12, 1855.

The enlightened woman of today bears love not only for her one man, but for mankind, not only for her own children, but all children.

Claudia Lady Bird Johnson
Speech, Kentucky Federation of
Women's Clubs Annual Convention,
Lexington, Kentucky, May 21, 1964.

Lyndon loved everybody, and a little bit more than half the world is women . . . [but] I do know he loved me most.

Claudia Lady Bird Johnson
Life, April 1995.

Love should be pure. / Harmless as pilgrims kisses on the shrine of Virgin Martyrs.

Dolley Madison
Verse sent to a Miss Edwards,
Washington, D.C., February 29, 1848.

You know I love you very much and would do anything in the world to please you, . . . I never could have loved anyone else, . . .

Edith Kermit Roosevelt
Letter to Theodore Roosevelt,
June 8, 1886.

. . . what e'er changes time may bring,/ I'll love thee as thou art!

Julia Gardiner Tyler
In a poem composed to her husband, John Tyler, on his sixty-second birthday, March 29, 1852.

. . . if my fondness serves, love,/ To gild those wreaths of thine,/ Then will thy path be marked, love,/ By radiance divine!

Julia Gardiner Tyler
In a poem composed for her husband on his sixty-fifth birthday, March 29, 1855.

This my pledge, dearest one, I will stand by you—not for duty, not for pity, not for honour—but for love—trusting, protecting, comprehending love. And no matter whether the wine be bitter or sweet we will share it together and find happiness in the comradeship.

Edith Wilson
Letter to Woodrow Wilson, September 19, 1915.

I love you as my own soul.

Ellen Axson Wilson
Letter to Woodrow Wilson, undated, 1884.

. . . it would be strange if a great love did not exert some great power upon one's life and nature.

Ellen Axson Wilson
Letter to Woodrow Wilson, April 3, 1885.

I could not love anyone whom I did not admire and look up to and believe in wholly . . .

Ellen Axson Wilson
Letter to Woodrow Wilson, May 12, 1885

I will at least try not to let myself be killed by excess love and joy.

Ellen Axson Wilson
Anticipating her husband's return
home; letter to Woodrow Wilson,
June 7, 1887.

Oh, how I adore you! I am perfectly sure that you are the greatest, most wonderful, most loveable man who ever lived. I am not expressing an opinion, I am simply stating a self-evident fact.

Ellen Axson Wilson
Letter to Woodrow Wilson,
July 28, 1913.

I idolize you,—love you till it hurts.

Ellen Axson Wilson
Letter to Woodrow Wilson,
July 29, 1913.

I love you, I adore you, in fact I'm mad about you. When, oh when am I to see you again?

Ellen Axson Wilson
Letter to Woodrow Wilson, July 30,
1913, while she was vacationing in
Cornish, New Hampshire

Loyalty

Oh, how I longed to put my arms 'round your neck and beg you to let me take part of the weariness, part of the responsibility and try to make you forget everything else in the assurance of love and loyalty that fills my heart.

Edith Wilson
Letter to Woodrow Wilson,
June 10, 1915.

Joseph McCarthy

What I think of Senator Joseph McCarthy can hardly be put into words. He is the greatest menace to freedom because he smears people without the slightest regard for the fact. Mr. McCarthy has played on our fears. The people who follow him don't know that they are destroying our democracy. We should be able to say whatever we want to say and think.

Eleanor Roosevelt
Comments following an address to students at City College, New York, September 20, 1951.

James Madison

Mr. Madison the fittest and one of the most sensible and candid of Virginians, a moral man unexceptionable in private life.

Abigail Adams
Letter to her daughter Abigail Adams Smith, March 18, 1808.

Mr. Madison was never temperate, but reasonably fond of generous diet and good wines tea and coffee.

Dolley Madison
Writings, May 15, 1839.

Man/Men

I am more and more convinced that man is a dangerous creature, and that power whether vested in many or a few is ever grasping, and like the grave cries, give, give.

Abigail Adams
Letter to John Adams
November 27, 1775

Do not put such unlimited power into the hands of the Husbands. Remember, all Men would be tyrants if they could, . . . That your Sex are Naturally Tyrannical is a Truth as thoroughly established as to admit of no dispute . . .

Abigail Adams
Letter to John Adams,
March 31, 1776.

I knew it was a man's world, but I needed to know. I'd be damned if I'd leave.

Rosalynn Carter
On attending cabinet meetings.
Comments at New York luncheon,
June 13, 1983.

Isn't that just like a man! He never gave me the slightest intimation of his intention! I had no idea!

Grace Coolidge
Remarks when she learned of her
husband's decision not to run for
reelection in 1928.

A man has to be encouraged. I think I told Ike every day how good I thought he was. Your ego has to be fed.

Mamie Eisenhower
Interview by Barbara Walters, *20/20
News Magazine*, ABC, October 1979.

I have always been surrounded by handsome men.

Florence Harding
Quoted, *The New York Times*,
April 25, 1923.

Men are such a combination of good and bad.

Jacqueline Kennedy
Quoted by Theodore H. White in
Life, December 6, 1963.

You men have the advantage of us women, in being able to go out, in the world and earning a living.

Mary Lincoln
Letter to Alexander Williamson,
November 10, 1867.

Manners

If we expect to inherit the blessings of our Fathers, we should return a little more to their primitive Simplicity of Manners, and not sink into inglorious ease.

Abigail Adams
Letter to John Adams,
October 16, 1774.

Marriage

. . . Sir if you please you may take me.

Abigail Adams
Letter to John Adams, October 4,
1784, saying she was ready to
become his wife.

. . . too early marriage will involve you in troubles that may render you & yours unhappy the remainder of your life.

Abigal Adams
Letter to her son John Quincy
Adams, November 7, 1790.

. . . I have tried not to be too controversial.

Barbara Bush
Her secret for a successful marriage,
to a group of women leaders,
Phoenix, Arizona, June 18, 1981.

I know a lot of wonderful men married to pills, and I know a lot of pills married to wonderful women, so one shouldn't judge that way.

Barbara Bush
Opposing Republican attacks on Bill Clinton which focused on his wife, Hillary Rodham Clinton. *Time*, August 24, 1992.

We developed a mutual respect from the very beginning of our marriage.

Rosalynn Carter
Interview, *U.S. News & World Report*, October 18, 1975.

. . . love him, honor, comfort and keep him . . .

Frances Cleveland
Not the tradional, "love, honor, and obey" vows when she married Grover Cleveland in the White House, June 2, 1886. Her husband changed the words.

I can wish the women of our country no better blessing than that their homes and their lives may be as happy and that their husbands may be as kind and attentive, considerate and affectionate, as mine.

Frances Cleveland
Letter, written June 3, 1888, to a correspondent in Providence, Rhode Island, denying the rumor that her husband was a wife-beater. Her letter was reprinted in several newspapers.

. . . This is not an arrangement or an understanding. This is a marriage. . . . You know, I'm not sitting here like some little woman standing by her man like Tammy Wynette. I'm sitting here because I love him and I respect him and I honor what he's been through and what we've been through together. . . .

Hillary Rodham Clinton
Defending her husband against infidelity charges; interview, *60 Minutes*, CBS, January 25, 1992.

I had no choice but to follow my heart.

Hillary Rodham Clinton
People, February 17, 1992.

Bill and I have always loved each other. No marriage is perfect, but just because it isn't perfect doesn't mean the only solution is to walk off and leave it. A marriage is always growing and changing.

Hillary Rodham Clinton
Glamour, August 1992.

We have been married for 22 years, . . . and I have learned a long time ago that the only people who matter in any marriage are the two that are in it.

Hillary Rodham Clinton
Interview, *Today, NBC-TV*,
January 27, 1998.

Our family was brought up on the fact that marriage is the greatest thing in the world.

Betty Ford
Comments to reporters, Vail,
Colorado, August 13, 1975.

My heart almost broke with the cruel thought that our marriage is based upon the cold, stern word duty.

Lucretia Garfield
Letter to James A. Garfield,
August 19, 1858.

When he spoke of marriage, I simply told him I thought it would be charming to be engaged, but to be married—no! I would rather be engaged.

Julia Dent Grant
The Personal Memoirs of Julia Dent Grant 1975.

Lyndon saw more in me than I saw in myself, and he expected more than I realized I could do.

Claudia Lady Bird Johnson
Reader's Digest, November 1963.

Marriage grows with the years. We survived so much together—so much good and so much bad. We were better together than apart.

Claudia Lady Bird Johnson
San Antonio Express, April 25, 1983.

Being married to a Senator, you have to adjust to the fact that the only routine is no routine.

Jacqueline Kennedy
Interview, *The New York Times*,
September 15, 1960.

I am married to a whirlwind.

Jacqueline Kennedy
Remark made during the 1959
primary election campaign.

. . . why is it that married folks always become so serious?

Mary Lincoln
Letter to Mary Ann Levering,
December 15, 1840.

It was always, music in my ears, both before & after our marriage, when my husband, told me, that I was the only one, he had ever thought of, or cared for.

Mary Lincoln
Letter to Mary Jane Welles,
October 6, 1865.

We've always been a team.

Patricia Pat Nixon
Interview with Virginia Sherwood,
ABC-TV, September 12, 1971.

I'm a woman who loves her husband, and I make no apologies for looking out for his personal and political welfare. We have a genuine, sharing marriage. I go to his aid. He comes to mine . . . We don't always agree. But neither marriage nor politics denies a spouse the right to hold an opinion or the right to express it. And if you have anything less, it's not marriage, it's servitude.

Nancy Reagan
Speech, annual Associated Press luncheon for the American Publishers Association, Washington, D.C., May 4, 1987.

Women who marry pass their best and happiest years in giving life and fostering it, meeting and facing the problems of the next generation and helping the universe to move . . .

Edith Kermit Roosevelt
Cleared for Strange Ports, 1927.

He never should have married me and then would have been free to make his own course . . .

Edith Kermit Roosevelt
Letter to her sister-in-law Anna Roosevelt Cowles, September 28, 1894, expressing remorse over her opposition to her husband's candidacy for mayor of New York.

. . . marriage is no longer the only aim and object in life, neither must you marry and have more or less the same kind of conditions which you were brought up in.

Eleanor Roosevelt
Radio talk to young women, December 16, 1932.

You may find the right man in Sunday School, or high school, or college. Staying married to him is another matter and the important thing.

Bess Truman
Quoted by Adela Rogers St. Johns, *Some Are Born Great*, 1974.

. . . as to the President [George Washington], he never has, nor ever will, as you have often heard him say, inter meddle in matrimonial concerns, . . .

Martha Washington
Letter to Fanny Bassett Washington,
September 29, 1794.

. . . the most remarkable life history that I ever even read about,— and to think I have lived it with you. I wonder if I am dreaming, and will wake up to find myself married to—a bank clerk,—say! I love you, my dear in every way you would wish to be loved,—deeply, tenderly, devotedly, passionately.

Ellen Axson Wilson
Letter to Woodrow Wilson,
October 5, 1913.

Media

The press never gets anything right.

Barbara Bush
Jesting at the Alfred E. Smith
Memorial Dinner, New York,
October 19, 1989.

Avoid this crowd like the plague. And if they quote you, make damn sure they heard you.

Barbara Bush
Advice to Hillary Rodham Clinton on
reporters covering the White House,
November 19, 1992. Mrs. Bush had
invited her successor for a tour of the
White House.

I hope you treat her as well as you treated me. I mean, give her a break.

Barbara Bush
Appealing to reporters to go easy on
the incoming First Lady, Hillary
Rodham Clinton. When a reporter
protested that "we haven't done
anything," Mrs. Bush shot back,
"ugly," of the media's portrayal of
Mrs. Clinton. White House,
December 1, 1992.

I just wish you people had a sense of humor. . . .

Barbara Bush
Comments while showing reporters
and photographers White House
Christmas decorations,
December 7, 1992.

The press is reporting things that should not be reported, in my opinion.

Barbara Bush
Former First Ladies Forum, Kennedy
Center, Washington, D.C.,
March 9, 1998.

. . . now the whole thing [The Washington Post] is a gossip column.

Barbara Bush
Her quip when Rosalynn Carter
noted that *The Washington Post*
ended its gossip column after the
Carters moved into the White
House. Former First Ladies Forum,
Kennedy Center, Washington, D.C.,
March 9, 1998.

It has been my unbroken policy not to see newspaper writers or give interviews to anyone. At the word interview spoken or written my ears go up and my chin out.

Grace Coolidge
Letter to Mrs. Reuben B. Hills,
circa 1928.

The papers used to really give us good material, and I think that has deteriorated.

Betty Ford
Former First Ladies Forum, Kennedy Center, Washington, D.C., March 9, 1998.

I love the newspaper fraternity. I'd tell them where to get a story and they'd get it and never mentioned me. I trusted them often and they never betrayed me.

Florence Harding
Comments to reporters covering the Republican National Convention, Chicago, June 12, 1920. [Mr. and Mrs. Warren G. Harding owned the Marion (Ohio) *Daily Star*.]

. . . I always take a particular interest in the activities of newspaper women, because I have regarded myself as quite one of them for a great many years.

Florence Harding
Letter to the New York Women's Newspaper Club, April 9, 1922.

Newswomen are a breed all of their own—hard-working, elastic, supersensitive to events, compassionate, not afraid to feel the human side of the situation, deeply sentimental, and usually blessed by a sense of humor.

Claudia Lady Bird Johnson
Remarks at the Women's National Press Club dinner, Washington, D.C., December 2, 1968.

. . . I think that they were better to me than I deserved and I think I left there [White House] with some good friends among them.

Claudia Lady Bird Johnson
Oral history interview, Lyndon Baines Johnson Library, January 23, 1987.

I'm so in love with all that world now—I think I look up to newspaper people the way you join movie star fan clubs when you're ten years old.

Jacqueline Kennedy
Letter to Bess Furman, 1952, when working as Inquiring Photographer at the *Washington Times-Herald.*

. . . I don't want to stereotype the press and I hope that the press won't try to stereotype me.

Nancy Reagan
Written comments, White House, October 12, 1981.

I feel that your position as I look upon it is to try to tell the women throughout the country what you think they should know. That, after all, is a newspaper woman's job, to make her impressions go to leading women in the country to form a general attitude of mind and thought.

Eleanor Roosevelt
Addressing the thirty-five women journalists who attended the first press conference held by a president's wife. White House, March 6, 1933.

Your job is an important one. . . . You are the interpreters to the women of the country as to what goes on politically in the legislative national life, and also what the social and personal life is at the White House.

Eleanor Roosevelt
Addressing the thirty-five women journalists who attended the first press conference held by a president's wife. White House, March 6, 1933.

Memories

I remember—who could forget?—the laughing hayrides and water-melon suppers, learning to swim in Mulberry Creek, the lazy curl of a cousin's fishing line flickering in the sun, church on Sunday and then the long Sunday dinner with kinfolks—endless kinfolk—discussing the endless gossip around the table.

Claudia Lady Bird Johnson
Speech, University of Alabama,
Tuscaloosa, February 25, 1966.

Memory is not a faithful servant. One year after, twenty years after, you may remember it washed over by the circumstances that came afterwards.

Claudia Lady Bird Johnson
Interview with Ted Koppel, *Nightline*,
ABC-TV, October 8, 1997.

Mental Health

As a nation, we are still running away from persons who have had or still have mental and emotional disorders. And the stigma attached to that plight is an undeserved disgrace.

Rosalynn Carter
Letter, *The New York Times*,
November 18, 1977.

All of us have had some stresses. . . . I'm sure that my children have more stresses than I ever had.

Rosalynn Carter
Testimony on mental health before
the Senate Resources Committee's
Subcommittee on Health and
Scientific Research,
February 7, 1979.

You're not healthy if you are mentally unhealthy. People who have mental illness have so many more physical illnesses than mentally healthy people have.

> **Rosalynn Carter**
> Interview, *The Washington Post*,
> June 24, 1993.

. . . mental illness ought to be considered just like a physical illness. If you're sick you're sick, and you ought to be able to get care and it's nothing to be ashamed of, for basically, mental illness is biological.

> **Rosalynn Carter**
> Former First Ladies Forum, Kennedy
> Center, Washington, D.C.,
> March 9, 1998.

Money

Debt and meanness is the penalty imposed by the salary of an American Minister.

> **Louisa Adams**
> Complaining about her husband's
> salary as American minister to Russia,
> in her diary, "The Adventures of a
> Nobody."

I always managed the money affairs of the family.

> **Mamie Eisenhower**
> Interview with Barbara Walters, *ABC*,
> March 26, 1970.

Never had any money to fight over.

> **Betty Ford**
> Interview, *60 Minutes*, *CBS*,
> August 10, 1975.

Don't you see how troublesome it is to carry around gold and silver?

Sarah Childress Polk
Remarks to her husband, President
James K. Polk, a staunch opponent of
the use of paper money as opposed
to gold and silver coins. Quoted in
Nelson and Nelson, *Memorials of
Sarah Childress Polk*, 1892.

Mamma says I must tell you that I am very practical and know a great deal about money.

Edith Kermit Roosevelt
Letter to Theodore Roosevelt,
June 8, 1886.

Please, dear Mr. McKim, don't think me very fussy and interfering; but I am very timid about money and I know what an enormous amount have been done on the White House beyond what strikes the eye, and the money must have gone like water. I do hate to write this, because I know how much you have the perfection of your work at heart, but I have felt that I must do so and I hope you will forgive me.

Edith Kermit Roosevelt
Letter to architect Charles McKim,
October 5, 1902. Mrs. Roosevelt
sought to control expenses of the
White House restoration work.

I have had the feeling that every penny I have made [from writing her newspaper column "My Day"] should be in circulation.

Eleanor Roosevelt
Press conference,
November 7, 1940.

We most of us [Missourians] know the value of a dollar or a dime for that matter.

Bess Truman
Quoted by Adela Rogers St. Johns,
Some Are Born Great, 1974.

Morals

Great Learning and superior abilities, should you ever possess them, will be of little value and small Estimation, unless Virtue, Honour, Truth and integrity are added to them.

Abigail Adams
Addressing her son John Quincy in a letter to John Adams, June 10, 1778.

Mother/Motherhood

I was a *Mother*. God had heard my prayer.

Louisa Adams
On the arrival of her first-born, George Washington Adams, born April 12, 1801.

It is horrible to be a man, but the grinding misery of being a woman between the upper and nether millstone of household cares and training children is almost as bad. To be half civilized with some aspirations for enlightenment and obliged to spend the largest part of the time the victim of young barbarians keeps one in perpetual ferment.

Lucretia Garfield
Letter to James A. Garfield, June 5, 1877.

. . . modern mother may build a home and at the same time have a career, preventing her from devoting all her time exclusively to the home.

Lou Henry Hoover
Toledo (Ohio) Times,
February 13, 1932.

When I was growing up I always expected to have children and lead an ordinary life. Except that really being a wife and a mother is not really ordinary. It's an extraordinary and fulfilling way of life to me.

Nancy Reagan
Speech, 5th Annual Joint Armed Forces Officers' Wives Luncheon, Washington, D.C., November 6, 1981.

It's the best thing I've ever done. Being a mother is what I think made me the person I am.

Jacqueline Kennedy Onassis
Quoted in Christopher Andersen,
Jackie After Jack, 1998.

I have often felt that I cheated my children a little. I was never so totally theirs as most mothers are. I gave to audiences what belonged to my children, got back from audiences the love my children longed to give to me.

Eleanor Roosevelt
Quoted by Liz Smith, *The Mother's Book*, 1978.

Music

I went last week to hear the musick in Westminster Abbey. The Messiah was performed. It was sublime beyond description.

Abigail Adams
Letter to Thomas Jefferson,
June 10, 1778.

Musick is a passion with me, and the love of it often makes me silly.

Louisa Adams
Quoted, Jack Shepherd, *Cannibals of the Heart*, 1980.

An engineer, a lawyer, a doctor, a teacher of classics, should be able to get much joy in life with a little more understanding of what music is all about than is just acquired by listening to the radio.

Lou Henry Hoover
Letter to Mrs. Baldwin, Friends of
Music, Stanford University,
August 14, 1937.

Of my own experience I can testify that "A Hot Time in the Old Town" makes a perfectly good funeral march when reduced to a measure sufficiently lugubrious.

Helen Taft
Recollections of Full Years, 1914.

. . . "The Star Spangled Banner" . . . is almost as difficult a tune to walk by as Mendelssohn's Wedding March . . .

Helen Taft
Referring to music played at official White House functions. *Recollections of Full Years*, 1914.

Name-Calling

He is a dirty dog.

Mary Lincoln
Letter to David Davis, March 6, 1867, on William H. Herndon, President Lincoln's former partner who presented lurid lectures on Lincoln's life and marriage.

I abominate ugly names—if they can be avoided.

Mary Lincoln
Letter to Sally Orne, November 7, 1869.

Mary Lincoln

Names

I long ago made peace with the nickname.

Claudia Lady Bird Johnson
Christened Claudia Alta Taylor when she was born, Mrs. Johnson has been called Lady Bird since she was two years old. Comments to reporters on her 51st birthday, December 22, 1963.

You are quite welcome to call me anything you please (even Eileen) except Ellie Lou. I have a decided dislike to that name—indeed, to all compound names.

Ellen Axson Wilson
Letter to Woodrow Wilson,
May 12, 1885.

Nature

. . . nature had given me more joy and serenity and good days and happy memories . . .

Claudia Lady Bird Johnson
Oral history interview, Lyndon Baines Johnson, October 10, 1990.

Necessity

Great necessities call out great virtues.

Abigail Adams
Letter to John Adams,
January 19, 1780.

New England

An unforgettable thing is to go to New England in the autumn and to fly over those gold and crimson and scarlet hills and valleys, dotted with lakes and enough green in it to serve as a foil. The trees reach like torches to the sky. I love driving through New England. It is breathtaking.

Claudia Lady Bird Johnson
Interview, *U.S. News & World Report*, February 22, 1965.

Richard M. Nixon

Of course he has matured through the years. But he wouldn't be worth his salt if he hadn't.

Patricia Pat Nixon
News conference, Chicago,
July 26, 1960.

I got the best guy in the world. I love him dearly.

Patricia Pat Nixon
News conference on jet plane during
presidential election campaign,
September 23, 1972.

Notoriety

A lady's name should appear in print only three times, at her birth, marriage, and death.

Edith Kermit Roosevelt
Her husband, Theodore Roosevelt,
explained to newsmen in 1898, that
this was her philosophy for refusing
to allow any pictures of herself and
her children to be published.

Nuts

It's nuts!

Hillary Rodham Clinton
Expressing her frustrations over
health care problems during a
speech in New Orleans, Louisiana,
March 4, 1993. Then, turning to
Louisiana Senator John Breaux, she
asked, "Is that a political term? Nuts?"

Obligations

All during my growing up years I had a combined message of personal opportunity [and] public responsibility—that there were obligations that people who were as lucky as I was owed society.

Hillary Rodham Clinton
Vanity Fair, May 1992.

I was raised to believe that every person had an obligation to take care of themselves, and their family. And that meant, you know, earning an income and saving and investing.

Hillary Rodham Clinton
News conference, White House,
April 22, 1994.

Obstinate

Mr. Grant was always a very obstinate man.

Julia Dent Grant
Telling a social guest that General
Grant would soon capture
Richmond. Ishbel Ross,
The General's Wife, 1959.

Olympics

These Olympic games, which have moved princes to lift peasants onto their shoulders, emphasize an inescapable dimension of the human experience—that we are all members of one global family.

Hillary Rodham Clinton
Speech, Olympia, Greece,
March 30, 1996.

Opinions

I tell him what I think and he tells me what he thinks, and then we are united.

Barbara Bush
On being candid with her husband;
press conference, Washington, D.C.,
January 14, 1989.

I do not speak out on issues because I am not the elected official. When I am an elected official, I will speak out and I hope George Bush will do for me what I have done for him.

Barbara Bush
Quoted, *Newsweek*,
January 23, 1989.

I, for better or worse, have spoken out on public issues for twenty-five years.

Hillary Rodham Clinton
Comments on the role of the First
Lady, George Washington University,
Washington, D.C.,
November 29, 1994.

. . . I do get angry about things. I'm not going to deny that. . . . And I'm not at all shy about expressing my opinion.

Hillary Rodham Clinton
Interview with Barbara Walters,
20/20, ABC, January 12, 1996.

I never thought being First Lady should prevent me from expressing my own opinions.

Betty Ford
NBC-TV, June 24, 1985.

I could tell you many curious things my brother, but as people say I have my opinions &, I must not trust my pen.

Dolley Madison
Letter to John G. Jackson,
April 10, 1811.

Although I don't get involved in policy, it's silly to suggest my opinions should not carry some weight with the man I've been married to for thirty-five years.

> **Nancy Reagan**
> Speech, annual Associated Press luncheon for the American Publishers Association, Washington, D.C., May 4, 1987.

Do your own thing. Don't be afraid to give your opinion. Just because you're married doesn't mean you've given up your rights to an opinion.

> **Nancy Reagan**
> Urging married women to be outspoken, interview, *Associated Press*, January 14, 1989.

Every woman is entitled to an opinion and the right to express an opinion—especially to the man she's married to.

> **Nancy Reagan**
> Interview, *CNN, The Larry King Show*, December 28, 1989.

You say that I dislike to give opinions. This is a lesson that will last my life, never to give it for it is utterly worthless when given,—worse than that in this case for it has helped to spoil some years of a life which I would have given my own for.

> **Edith Kermit Roosevelt**
> Letter to her sister-in-law Anna Roosevelt Cowles, September 28, 1894, on her opposition to her husband's candidacy for Mayor of New York.

Opportunity

Your horizons are not finite. You were born at the right time. It is a good time to be a woman. It is a good time to be alive.

> **Claudia Lady Bird Johnson**
> Speech, Texas Woman's University, Denton, Texas, March 31, 1964.

Anyone with imagination, zeal and brains has many opportunities in unfinished America.

Claudia Lady Bird Johnson
Speech, Radcliffe College,
Cambridge, Massachusetts,
June 9, 1964.

You must prepare to grasp every opportunity which comes to you. We cannot rebuke ourselves for what we have no chance to do. Most of us are creatures of circumstances, limited in the opportunities which come to us, and the only thing in life which we may be justly proud is that we have not let those opportunities which have been given us, slide.

Eleanor Roosevelt
Speech, Cornell University, Ithaca,
New York, October 23, 1937.

Oratory

If you speak to the mass of the people as though you were talking to any one individual in your living room, you will reach their hearts and that is all that you have to bother about.

Eleanor Roosevelt
Advice to Adlai Stevenson,
October 10, 1956.

Pain

How I did long for your tender fingers last night to rub away the pain in my eyes.

Edith Wilson
Letter to Woodrow Wilson,
August 5, 1915.

Painter

I had always had the greatest desire to be a painter . . .

Ellen Axson Wilson
Trenton Evening Times,
January 8, 1913.

Palestine

I think that it will be in the long-term interest of the Middle-East for Palestine to be a state and for it to be a state that is responsible for its citizens' well-being, a state that has responsibility for providing education and health care and economic opportunity for its citizens, a state that has to accept the responsibility of governing.

Hillary Rodham Clinton
Remarks made via satellite to a group
of Arab and Israeli youth meeting in
Villars, Switzerland, May 6, 1998

Parents/Parenting

To your parents you owe Love, reverence and obedience to all just and equitable commands.

Abigail Adams
Letter to her son John Quincy Adams,
March 20, 1780.

. . . whilst our parents live, we cannot feel unprotected. To them we can apply for advice and direction, sure that it will be given with affection and tenderness.

Abigail Adams
Letter to her daughter Abigail
"Nabby" Adams, January 25, 1791.

Everybody is down on people on welfare, but the neglect of children, absentee parents is not confined to welfare parents.

Hillary Rodham Clinton
White House luncheon with women
reporters, January 9, 1995.

. . . I know it is infinitely tougher for most women who every day are trying to do the best they can, and I honestly don't know how single parents do it. And I think we ought to be very sympathetic and very supportive of all parents, but particularly of single parents.

Hillary Rodham Clinton
Speech, University of Maryland,
College Park, Maryland,
October 3, 1997.

I have often thought that being a parent is the most important thing we are given to do.

Nancy Reagan
Remarks during a visit to a St.
Petersburg (Florida) elementary
school, February 15, 1982.

Being a parent is the greatest challenge we have in life and the one for which we have no training at all.

Nancy Reagan
Speech, Alabama Governor's
Conference on Drug Awareness,
Montgomery, Alabama,
September 27, 1982.

I tried to be a good mother. I don't think anybody's perfect, but then, you know, there's no perfect parent—there's no perfect child.

Nancy Reagan
Barbara Walters Special, ABC,
March 24, 1986.

Paris

. . . nobody ever leaves paris [sic] but with a degree of tristeness.

Abigail Adams
Letter to Thomas Jefferson,
June 6, 1785.

Partners

Jimmy and I were always partners. We campaigned as a team. We were a team in the White House.

Rosalynn Carter
Comments at a New York luncheon,
June 13, 1983.

We care about the same issues and values and concerns. We are a partnership.

Hillary Rodham Clinton
People, February 17, 1992.

Much as I love your delicious love letters, . . . I believe I enjoy even more the ones in which you tell me . . . of what you are working on—the things that fill your thoughts and demand your best effort, for then I feel I am sharing your work and being taken into partnership as it were.

Edith Wilson
Letter to Woodrow Wilson,
June 18, 1915.

Passion

Time will dim the Lusture of the Eye, and wither the bloom of the face, tho it may perfect and mature those mental attractions which yield a more permanent and solid satisfaction, when the ardour of passion settles into a more lasting union of Friendship.

Abigail Adams
Letter to John Quincy Adams,
February 29, 1795.

The passions are like sounds of nature, only heard in her solitudes. Our senses may captivate us with beauty, but in absence we can forget or by reason we can conquer so superficial an impression; our vanity may enamour us with rank, but the affections of vanity are traced in sand; but who can love genius and not feel that the sentiments it excites partake of its own intenseness and its own immortality.

Dolley Madison
Statement found in an album of her
sister, Anna Payne Cutts.

Patriotism

Tough certain pains attend the cares of State A Good Man owes his Country to be great.

Abigail Adams
Letter to Mercy Otis Warren,
April 27, 1776.

Justice, humanity and Benevolence are the duties you owe to society in general. To your Country the same duties are incumbent upon you with the additional obligation of sacrificing ease, pleasure, wealth and life itself for its defence and security.

Abigail Adams
Letter to John Quincy Adams,
March 20, 1780.

All history and every age exhibit instances of patriotismic virtue in the female sex which, considering our situation, equals the most heroic of yours. . . . When you offer your blood to the state—it is ours—on giving it our sons and husbands we give more than ourselves—you can only die in the field of battle -but we have the misfortune to survive those whom we love the most.

Abigail Adams
Letter to John Adams, June 17, 1782.

. . . make the next generation a little bit more honest about what the word [patriotism] means. We must teach them that it is not just to say your country is always right, or that it is always the greatest country in the world, but that it is the desire to make our country stand for all the things you feel are right, and to fight for that ideal.

Eleanor Roosevelt
Speech, Women's Club of New York,
January 5, 1933.

What a glorious country is America! Who can recount such deeds of courage and valor as our countrymen?

Julia Gardiner Tyler
Expressing her patriotism during the
war with Mexico in 1846–1848.

Peace

We know we can lead in war. We are leading in peace.

Hillary Rodham Clinton
Speech to American troops working
as peacekeepers in Bosnia-
Herzegovina. Markovici,
March 25, 1996.

Everywhere, peace is uppermost in women's minds. They say if we can't keep the peace, then the other issues aren't important. Not one woman called upon, put the budget ahead of peace.

Jacqueline Kennedy
Discussing presidential campaign
issues. Interview by Henry Fonda,
CBS-TV, November 2, 1960.

It isn't enough to talk about peace. One must believe in it. And it isn't enough to believe in it. One must work at it.

Eleanor Roosevelt
In a Voice of America broadcast,
November 11, 1951.

. . . peace, like freedom, is elusive, hard to come by, harder to keep. It cannot be put into a purse or a hip pocket and buttoned there to stay.

Eleanor Roosevelt
Speech, Democratic National
Convention, Chicago, July 22, 1952.

We must endeavor to let our ways be the way of pleasantness and all our paths Peace.

Martha Washington
Letter to Annis Stockton Boudinot,
January 15, 1794.

People

There is a song from one of our not new musical comedies about girls, which says something about "the short, the fat, the lean, the tall; I don't give a rap, I love them all." This is the way I feel about people, and I have been fortunate in being placed where I had an opportunity to gratify my taste by meeting great numbers of them.

> **Grace Coolidge**
> Explaining her feelings about people.
> Mrs. Coolidge's good humor and
> love of people acted as a buffer to
> her husband's stiffness and silence.

These [political] trips are not hard on me because I enjoy people.

> **Patricia Pat Nixon**
> *New York Times Magazine*,
> October 30, 1960.

Perfection

There isn't any perfect human institution. There is no perfect market except in the abstract theories of economists. There is no perfect government except in the dreams of political leaders. And there is no perfect society. We have to work with human beings as we find them.

> **Hillary Rodham Clinton**
> Speech before the World Economic
> Forum, Davos, Switzerland,
> February 2, 1998.

Perseverance

Great difficulties may be surmounted, by patience and perseverance.

> **Abigail Adams**
> Letter to John Adams,
> November 27, 1775.

Philosophy

I am one of those who are willing to rejoice always. My disposition and habits are not of the gloomy kind. I believe that to enjoy is to obey.

Abigail Adams
Letter to Caroline Smith,
November 22, 1812.

. . . my philosophy is that you do what you have to do.

Rosalynn Carter
New York Times Magazine,
March 20, 1977.

Before I get out of bed, I take a moment to appreciate the day I have.

Betty Ford
Los Angeles Times,
November 12, 1995.

If I have a philosophy, it would resolve itself into an effort not to make everybody suffer unnecessarily.

Eleanor Roosevelt
Talk at Sinai Temple, Chicago,
November 16, 1936.

Physical Fitness

I would wish you often either ride, or walk out, as I think it be conducive to health, . . .

Anna Harrison
Letter to her son William,
May 8, 1819.

I am a firm believer in the theory that you cannot have the best functions of a good mind without a good body. The body must be developed along with the mind.

Lou Henry Hoover
Comments while visiting the Physical
Education Department of Goucher
College, Baltimore, Maryland,
October 30, 1931.

Politician

I became an enthusiastic politician.

Julia Dent Grant
On her husband's nomination for the
presidency, 1868. *The Personal
Memoirs of Julia Dent Grant*,1975.

A politician ought to be born a foundling and remain a bachelor.

Claudia Lady Bird Johnson
Time, December 1, 1975.

. . . I became quite a politician, rather an unladylike profession.

Mary Lincoln
Letter to Mercy Ann Levering,
December 1840.

You know I am not much of a politician, but I am anxious to hear (as
far as you think proper) what is going forward in the Cabinet.

Dolley Madison
Letter to James Madison,
November 1, 1805.

If a politician is considered a public servant unselfishly giving his time
to carrying out the wishes of the majority of the people, you could
hardly look down upon a politician.

Eleanor Roosevelt
White House press conference,
March 25, 1935.

Politics

I cannot wean myself from the subject of politicks.

Abigail Adams
Letter to Catherine Johnston,
May 8, 1810.

There are some silly plans going on here, and God only knows in what they will end, but I fear not at all to my taste.

Louisa Adams
Commenting on her husband's plan to seek election to the House of Representative after having served as the nation's sixth president. Letter to her son, John Adams 2nd, October 1, 1830.

I am not very sympathetic with the theory that political wives have a hard time. I think it really depends upon the husband.

Barbara Bush
Interview, *The New York Times*, February 22, 1981.

I am a political person. I've always said I'm more political than Jimmy. I'm political, he's not. I care what happens. I'll say, "You've got to do this," and he says, "We've got to do what's right."

Rosalynn Carter
Speech, New York Women in Communications Inc., New York, March 26, 1979.

I think the city of Washington itself is insular to a certain extent. You have to get out in the country to realize what is going on and discover that the perceptions in Washington aren't necessarily accurate.

Rosalynn Carter
Comments at book luncheon, Washington, D.C., April 12, 1984.

We're always looking for candidates that have new approaches to problems.

Rosalynn Carter
PBS, September 4, 1990.

I would advise any young person to go into politics. [It is] Hard. Not easy. . . . We need good people in politics so bad.

Rosalynn Carter
Former First Ladies Forum, Kennedy Center, Washington, D.C., March 9, 1998.

For too long, those who lead us have viewed politics as the art of the possible. The challenge that faces them—and us—now is to practice politics as the art of making possible what appears impossible.

Hillary Rodham Clinton
Commencement speech, Wellesley
College, Wellesley, Massachusetts,
May 31, 1969.

. . . the political climate in our country today is kind of difficult.

Hillary Rodham Clinton
Comments to reporters, Lebanon,
New Hampshire, January 25, 1996.

I believe in the balance of power. I believe in the balance of power in government. I believe in the balance of power between the government and private sector. I believe in the balance of power between men and women. And I believe if you tilt too far in one way or the other, you get in trouble.

Hillary Rodham Clinton
On her political philosophy, White
House awards ceremony,
January 30, 1997.

Well, we are all interested in politics—we should be. But I am not actively interested.

Grace Coolidge
Comments to reporters upon arriving
home after a six-month absence,
August 1936.

Politics is Jerry's life, and I like it, too.

Betty Ford
Interview, *The New York Times*,
October 15, 1973.

I am perfectly willing to tackle a political issue as long as it doesn't disturb my husband and he didn't step on my toes.

Betty Ford
60 Minutes, ABC, August 10, 1975.

I think that today there is a lot more bitterness in politics.

Betty Ford
Former First Ladies Forum, Kennedy
Center, Washington, D.C.,
March 9, 1998.

Surely we women will not permit it ever to be said that because we came into full obligation of citizenship our contribution served to lower the standard of civic responsibility. Rather, we must seek credit for raising those standards, for attaching the nation yet more firmly to the fundamentals of sound policy, the verities of good government and of the ideal of greatest service to the greatest number.

Florence Harding
Letter to Mrs. Arthur L. Livermore,
president of the Women's National
Republican Club, January 14, 1922.

Your ignorance of politics is not a grave offense. You could not expect to know and enjoy politics as I do.

Lucy Hayes
Explaining politics to her son,
Birchard Austin Hayes.

Sometimes I think I am tired of Politics and then again it is pleasant.

Lucy Hayes
Letter to her brother James D. Webb,
August 9, 1869.

Women should get into politics. They should take a more active part in civic affairs, give up some of their time devoted to pleasure for their duty as citizens. Whether we are wanted in politics or not, we are here to stay, and the only force that can put us out of politics is that which gave us the vote. The vote itself is not a perfect utility. It is perfected in the way in which it is used.

Lou Henry Hoover
Speech, annual meeting of the
Republican Women of Pennsylvania,
Philadelphia, May 4, 1923.

I would hate for you to go into politics.

Claudia Lady Bird Johnson
Letter written in October 1934 to
Lyndon B. Johnson after he had
proposed marriage. They were
married in November 1934.

I always hope that the very best of our people will go into politics,
and I am sure that some of our best are women.

Claudia Lady Bird Johnson
Speech, National Convention of
American Home Economics
Association, Detroit, June 24, 1964.

. . . I have never thought of myself as a political person . . . But . . . I
have come to respect and love our party . . . of the people . . .

Claudia Lady Bird Johnson
Speech, Kentucky Democratic
Women's Club, Louisville,
October 5, 1968.

I don't know anything about politics, or didn't until after I got married.
Then I heard so much of it all around me all the time that I learned
about politics through a kind of osmosis.

Jacqueline Kennedy
Comments made during the
presidential election campaign, 1960.

I scarcely know, how I would bear up, under defeat.

Mary Lincoln
Letter to Hannah Shearer,
October 20, 1860, referring to the
presidential election of
November 6, 1860.

Poilitics is the business of men. I don't care what offices they may
hold, or who supports them. I care only about people.

Dolley Madison
Comments in a letter to her sister.
Cited in Paul F. Boller, Jr., *Presidential
Wives*, 1988.

In political life you can't count on anything.

> **Patricia Pat Nixon**
> News conference, San Francisco,
> August 20, 1956.

I can think of any number of things I prefer to politics.

> **Patricia Pat Nixon**
> News conference, San Francisco,
> August 20, 1956.

I could see that it was the life he [Richard M. Nixon] wanted, so I told him that it was his decision, and I would do what he liked.

> **Patricia Pat Nixon**
> *Time*, February 29, 1960.

My husband attends to the political end.

> **Patricia Pat Nixon**
> *The New York Times*,
> October 30, 1960.

Politics is a funny business, you're up one day, down the next.

> **Patricia Pat Nixon**
> *Time*, October 9, 1972.

I have sacrificed everything in my life that I consider precious in order to advance the political career of my husband.

> **Patricia Pat Nixon**
> Quoted in Betty Medsger, *Women at Work*, 1975.

Oh how I wish he [Franklin Pierce] was out of political life! How much better it would be for him on every account!

> **Jane Pierce**
> Letter written while Franklin Pierce
> served as a U.S. Senator, June 1836.

You & I do most cordially hate politics—and it is difficult to know amidst the various opinions . . . will tend most to the good of our beloved country . . .

> **Jane Pierce**
> Letter to Mary Aiken, March 29, 1860.

Obviously we talk politics all the time.

> **Nancy Reagan**
> *The New York Times*, April 5, 1986.

Politics are seething abominably.

> **Edith Kermit Roosevelt**
> When her husband was attacking the
> policies of President Taft; letter to her
> son Kermit Roosevelt,
> undated, 1910.

We must . . . remember that the great power of the women to make themselves felt lies in their power to help select at the primaries, not only candidates for elective offices, but the officials of their county political organizations.

> **Eleanor Roosevelt**
> Speech, state convention of the
> New York Democratic Party, Albany,
> New York, April 14, 1924.

American women are backward about taking a serious and active part in politics. They have the vote, they have the power, but they don't seem to know what to do with it.

> **Eleanor Roosevelt**
> Interview, *The New York Times*,
> April 20, 1924.

If it's a man's game so decidedly that a woman would be soiled by entering it, then there is something radically wrong with the American game of politics.

> **Eleanor Roosevelt**
> Interview, *The New York Times*,
> April 20, 1924.

. . . if women believe they have a right and duty in political life today, they must learn to talk the language of men. They must not only master the phraseology, but also understand the machinery which men have built up through years of practical experience. Against the men bosses there must be women bosses who can talk as equals, with the backing of a coherent organization of women voters behind them.

Eleanor Roosevelt
Article, "Women Must Learn to Play the Game as Men Do," *Redbook*, April 1928.

The President doesn't discuss these things with me. Many people think that he does, but most often the first I know of some decision is when I see it in the papers.

Eleanor Roosevelt
Remarking to reporters in Dayton, Ohio, July 11, 1944, that her husband's decision to accept a fourth-term nomination for president was news to her.

A woman [entering politics] has to be prepared to take all that men take and a little more, because here we believe that all is fair in love and politics. Men can stand up under whispering campaigns a little better than women, because we still feel women should have a different kind of reputation than men.

Eleanor Roosevelt
Address to the Foreign Press Association, New York, May 23, 1947.

. . : of course, it was fun to win.

Bess Truman
Comments to reporters after the Democratic National Convention had nominated her husband, Harry S. Truman, to be the vice presidential nominee; Chicago, July 22, 1944.

Everything in the political world is calculated to interest me . . .

Julia Gardiner Tyler
Letter to her mother, Juliana
Gardiner, February 3, 1861.

. . . experience has taught me that politics is not the best school for the propagation of the purest code of morals!

Julia Gardiner Tyler
"Reminiscences of Mrs. Julia G.
Tyler," *Cincinnati Graphic News*,
June 25, 1887.

. . . we have not a single article of news but pollitick which I do not concern myself about.

Martha Washington
Letter to Fanny Bassett Washington,
February 25, 1788.

Sarah Childress Polk

I don't see or hear that Mrs. Polk is making any sensation in Washington.

Julia Gardiner Tyler
Catty remark about her successor at
the White House; letter to Margaret
Gardiner, February 5, 1846.

Poverty

Could we have the vision of doing away in this great country with poverty? . . . . what can make us not only the nation that has some of the richest people in the world, but the nation where there are no people that have to live at a substandard level. That could be one of the very best arguments against Communism that we could possibly have.

Eleanor Roosevelt
Speech, Democratic National
Convention, August 13, 1956.

Power

I can not say that I think you very generous to the Ladies, for whilst you are proclaiming peace and good will to Men, Emancipating all Nations, you insist upon retaining an absolute power over Wives. But you must remember that Arbitrary power is like most other things which are very hard, very liable to be broken—and notwithstanding all your wise Laws and Maxims we have it in our power not only to free ourselves but to subdue our Masters, and without violence throw both your natural and legal authority at our feet . . .

Abigail Adams
Letter to John Adams, May 7, 1776.

. . . extraordinary power is unleashed when women reach out to their neighbors and find common ground, when they begin to lift themselves up and by doing so lift up their families, their neighbors and their communities.

Hillary Rodham Clinton
Speech, University of Ulster, Belfast,
Northern Ireland, October 31, 1997.

How men hate a woman in a position of real power!

Eleanor Roosevelt
Response to Secretary of Labor,
Frances Perkins, who had com-
plained about her troubles at the
Department of Labor. Quoted in
Joseph P. Lash, *Love Eleanor*, 1982.

Pragmatism

I've always thought of myself as a pragmatist because a lot of what I believe we should do for one another is very practical.

Hillary Rodham Clinton
Newsweek, January 15, 1996.

. . . the only way now to get along is to take the world as you find it and make the best of it. It will be the means of satisfying your feelings much better than by showing them your dislike or opposition. That is the way to triumph and make your enemies even speak well of you.

Julia Gardiner Tyler
Letter to her son Lyon, attending the University of Virginia, January 1873.

Julia Gardiner Tyler

Prayers

My thoughts and my meditations are with you, though personally absent; and my petitions to Heaven are, that "the things which make for peace may not be hidden from your eyes." My feelings are not those of pride or ostentation, upon the occasion. They are solemnized by a sense of the obligations, the important trusts, and numerous duties connected with it. That you may be enabled to discharge them with honor to yourself, with justice and impartiality to your country, and with satisfaction to this great people, shall be the daily prayer of your A. A.

Abigail Adams
Letter to John Adams, February 8, 1797, as he is inaugurated as the second president of the United States.

President/Presidency

I thoroughly expect to vote for a woman President in my lifetime.

Barbara Bush
Interview, *The New York Times*, April 8, 1984.

So I offer you today a new legend: the winner of the hoop race will be the first to realize her dream . . . not society's dream . . . her own personal dream. And who knows? Somewhere out in this audience may even be someone who will one day follow my footsteps, and preside over the White House as the President's spouse. I wish him well!

> **Barbara Bush**
> Commencement address, Wellesley College, Wellesley, Massachusetts, June 1, 1990.

You may think the President is all-powerful, but he is not. He needs a lot of guidance from the Lord.

> **Barbara Bush**
> Speech to schoolchildren, January 7, 1991.

I have tried to keep in mind that the President is the image of God and therefore perfect, and this is most comforting to me. [Following President Eisenhower's heart attack.]

> **Mamie Eisenhower**
> Letter to Joshena Ingersol, September 29, 1955.

I think a president has to be able to think like the people think.

> **Betty Ford**
> Quoted, Walleschinsky and Wallace, *The People's Almanac*, 1975.

. . . I cannot see why anyone should want to be President in the next four years. I can see but one word written over the head of my husband if he is elected, and that word is "Tragedy."

> **Florence Harding**
> Comments to reporters at the Republican nominating convention, Chicago, June 10, 1920.

Well, Warren Harding, I have got you the Presidency; what are you going to do with it?

> **Florence Harding**
> Soon after the Hardings arrived at the White House, a member of the office staff overheard Mrs. Harding teasing her husband.

I wish that my husband's friends had left him where he is, happy and contented in retirement.

> **Anna Harrison**
> Comments at the news of her husband's [William Henry Harrison] landslide electoral victory in 1840.

Well, Mamie, your father's got it.

> **Caroline Harrison**
> To her daughter Mary (affectionately known as "Mamie") when she learned that her husband, Benjamin Harrison, had been elected president in 1888.

. . . I am glad of it for Mr. Jackson's sake, because it is his ambition. For me it is but one more burden. Even if I was qualified in other ways to do the honors of the White House, my health is not good enough to bear the strain.

> **Rachel Jackson**
> Comments to General William Carroll who, on December 9, 1828, brought her news that General Andrew Jackson had been elected president. Long in ill health, Mrs. Jackson died December 22, 1828, as she made preparations to follow her husband to Washington.

I really think it was a bad law [the two-term limitation for presidents] . . . I think that should be left to the people to decide whether they want someone to run for a third term . . .

> **Nancy Reagan**
> Interview with Helen Thomas, *United Press International*, White House, December 11, 1985.

If I wanted to be selfish, I could wish that he [Franklin D. Roosevelt] had not been elected.

> **Eleanor Roosevelt**
> Quoted by Lorena Hickok,
> November 9, 1932.

I do not think that we have yet reached the point where the majority of our people would feel satisfied to follow the leadership and trust the judgment of a woman as President.

> **Eleanor Roosevelt**
> Radio broadcast, NBC,
> September 4, 1934.

. . . sure there will be a woman President some day, but that day is not yet here. We women have to prove ourselves and at the present moment I do not think the country as a whole would have enough confidence in a woman, and without that confidence and coopera- tion she could not do a good job.

> **Eleanor Roosevelt**
> Radio talk, *NBC*, June 16, 1937.

What kind of people does this country want in the White House? . . . Women who give up everything? But you don't elect the woman nor the family when you elect a man President.

> **Eleanor Roosevelt**
> White House press conference,
> December 19, 1938.

Is there anything we can do for you? For you are the one in trouble now.

> **Eleanor Roosevelt**
> Remarks to Harry S. Truman, April
> 12, 1945, upon the death of
> President Franklin D. Roosevelt.

A woman would have no chance at all to be elected [president of the United States]. And what is more, I wouldn't wish it on her. If by some fluke a woman was nominated and elected, she could not hold her following.

> **Eleanor Roosevelt**
> Address before the Foreign Press
> Association, New York, May 23, 1947.

From a personal standpoint, I did not want my husband to be president. I realized, however, that it was impossible to keep a man out of public service when that was what he wanted and was undoubtedly well equipped for. It was pure selfishness on my part, and I never mentioned my feelings on the subject to him. . . .

Eleanor Roosevelt
Expressing her feelings about her husband's decision to run for president in 1932. *This I Remember*, 1949.

It isn't really possible under our system, I fear, for the Executive and the Legislature to get along well.

Eleanor Roosevelt
Letter to Joseph Lash,
August 23, 1952.

When we elect a President and a Vice President we must be prepared to face the fact that the Vice President may become President.

Eleanor Roosevelt
Meet the Press, NBC,
September 16, 1956.

Make it the presidency.

Helen Taft
Mrs. Taft's quip when, during a 1906 party at the White House, President Theodore Roosevelt played the part of a fortune teller, saying a man [William Howard Taft] in the room was destined to get the presidency or a chief justiceship.

We are not any one of us happy to be where we are but there's nothing to be done about it except to do our best—and forget about the sacrifices and many unpleasant things that bob up.

Bess Truman
Commenting on Harry S. Truman's succession to the presidency; letter to Mary Paxton Kesley, her childhood friend from Independence, Missouri, May 12, 1945.

I cannot blame him for having acted according to his ideas of duty in obeying the voice of his country.

Martha Washington
Letter to Mercy Otis Warren, December 26, 1789, on her husband's decision to accept the presidency.

Press Secretary

What is a press secretary for—to help the press, yes—but also to protect us.

Jacqueline Kennedy
Memo to the President's Press Secretary, Pierre Salinger, after one magazine published unauthorized photographs of her children.

Priorities

If you are doing too many things at once you will lose the drive that is necessary [to achieve your goal].

Eleanor Roosevelt
Address to the National Council of Negro Women's Interracial Conference, November 16, 1956.

Privacy

There isn't a person watching this who would feel comfortable sitting on this couch detailing everything that ever went on in their life or their marriage. And I think it's real dangerous in this country if we don't have some zone of privacy for everybody. I mean, I think that is absolutely critical.

Hillary Rodham Clinton
Discussing her marriage and infidelity charges against her husband; *60 Minutes*, CBS, January 25, 1992.

I am a Private Person.

Bess Truman
Quoted by Adela Rogers St. Johns,
Some Are Born Great, 1974.

Procrastination

. . . my evil genius Procrastination has whispered me to tarry til a
more convenient season . . .

Mary Lincoln
Letter to Mercy Ann Levering,
June 1841.

Progress

. . . progress is made by each generation recognizing what has been
achieved for good by the last generation, . . . and striving to preserve
and adapt these as a basis for further improvement. . . .

Lou Henry Hoover
"Let's Talk It Over Hour" broadcast,
NBC.

Prosperity

. . . where women prosper, countries prosper.

Hillary Rodham Clinton
Speech, Istanbul, Turkey,
March 27, 1996.

Public Affairs

What knowledge I had of public affairs I obtained from the daily
papers and other sources of information open to everybody.

Grace Coolidge
Autobiographical article, *American
Magazine*, August 1929.

Publicity

Accustomed as I had been for years to publicity, yet it became a sort of shock to me that nearly everything I did [as First Lady], and especially my slightest innovation, had what the reporters call "news value."

> **Helen Taft**
> *Reflections of Full Years*, 1914.

Public Life

I expect to be vilified and abused with my whole family when I come into this situation . . .

> **Abigail Adams**
> Letter to her sister Mary Cranch,
> June 3, 1797.

You see, dear Birch, without intending to be public [a public figure], I find myself for a quiet, "mind her own business" woman rather notorious.

> **Lucy Hayes**
> Letter to her son Birchard Austin
> Hayes, May 19, 1877, referring to
> criticism of the White House
> temperance policy.

. . . if you are in public life . . . your main effort is to make it [a] comfortable, peaceful place for your husband to work and prepare— just carry all the heavy load of public life.

> **Claudia Lady Bird Johnson**
> Oral history interview, Lyndon Baines
> Johnson Library, October 10, 1990.

It's all very well for those who like it, but I do not like this public life at all. I often wish the time would come when we would return to where I feel we best belong.

> **Eliza Johnson**
> Quoted by W. H. Crook, *Memoirs of
> the White House: Personal Reflections
> of Colonel* W. H. Crook, 1911.

I felt as though I had just turned into a piece of public property. It's frightening to lose your anonymity at thirty-one.

Jacqueline Kennedy
Comments made at her husband's inauguration, Washington, D.C., January 20, 1961.

I think that the public must be as sick of hearing about us . . . as I am.

Jacqueline Kennedy
Ladies Home Journal, October 1962.

I'm a mother, I'm a wife. I am not a public official.

Jacqueline Kennedy
Quoted, Richard Reeves, *President Kennedy*, 1993.

One hates to feel that all one's life is public property.

Edith Kermit Roosevelt
Undated letter to her daughter Anna Roosevelt Cowles.

I think it was much too late for him to go into publick life again, but it was not to be avoided, our family will be deranged as I must soon follow him.

Martha Washington
Letter to John Dandridge, April 20, 1789, referring to George Washington being elected President.

. . . I have too much of the vanity of human affairs to expect felicity from the splended scenes of public life. I am still determined to be cheerful and to be happy in whatever situation I may be; for I have also learned from experience that the greater part of our happiness or misery depends upon our disposition, and not upon our circumstances. We carry the seeds of the one or the other about with us in our minds wherever we go.

Martha Washington
Letter to Mercy Otis Warren, December 26, 1789.

Public Schools

We [the Hoovers] . . . believe that the democratic influence of a good public school in a good community gives a much better training than the unavoidable exclusiveness of even the best private schools.

Lou Henry Hoover
Letter to Senator Frank B. Kellogg,
March 1, 1922.

Public Service

Popular governments are peculiarly liable to factions, to cabals, to intrigue, to the juggling tricks of party, and the people may often be deceived for a time, by some fair speaking demagogue, but they will never be deceived long; and though they may, in a moment of excitement, sanction an injustice toward an old and faithful servant, they appreciate his worth, and hand his name down with honor to posterity, even though that "name may not be agreeable to the fashionable." It is one which I take a pride in bearing, and one that I hope and pray my children may never dishonor.

Louisa Adams
In a letter to John Quincy Adams,
describing her feelings about his
public service.

What I'm interested in . . . is called public service. I have a deep, abiding sense of obligation that makes it very hard for me to see the waste and the damage and the hurt that occur every day. I can't help want to do everything about it.

Hillary Rodham Clinton
Glamour, August 1992.

I don't think there's any point in being in public service if you don't really believe that you want to make a difference to help people.

Hillary Rodham Clinton
The Baltimore Sun,
September 4, 1992.

Quaker Society

This lecture [by two ladies who thought she had too many visitors during her illness in Philadelphia] made me recollect the times when our Society used to control me entirely and debar me from so many advantages and pleasures, and although so entirely from their clutches, I really felt my ancient terror of them revive to a disagreeable degree.

Dolley Madison
Letter to Anna Cutts,
August 19, 1805.

Racism

We have racism in our country and we've got to do away with it.

Barbara Bush
Press conference, White House,
January 16, 1990.

People overlook the importance of forcing this conversation. The black-and-white issue has to be the focus because it's the unfinished business of America. But I think we can help people understand it better if they see it as part of the overall dilemma of bigotry and prejudice that we have to contend with.

Hillary Rodham Clinton
Comments at an event sponsored by
the Team Harmony Foundation to
help school children combat bigotry;
Boston, Massachusetts, December 9,
1997.

It would be bottomless tragedy for our country to be racially divided and here I want to say emphatically, this is not a challenge only in the South. It is a national challenge—in the big cities of the North as in the South.

Claudia Lady Bird Johnson
Campaign speech, Alexandria,
Virginia, October 6, 1964.

Reading

Have you ever tried something that was really hard to do? How about reading? You have to keep practicing over and over again, . . . when you are learning to read.

Hillary Rodham Clinton
Advice to students at Garrison
Elementary School, Washington, D.C.,
February 26, 1997.

Reading to her [daughter Chelsea] when she was young was a joy for Bill and me. But we had no idea fifteen, sixteen, seventeen years ago that what we were doing was literally turning on the power in her brain, firing up the connections that would enable her to speak and read at as high level as she possibly could reach.

Hillary Rodham Clinton
White House news conference on
child rearing, April 17, 1997.

I wish you could read to me as you frequently have done after I sit down to sewing.

Abigail Fillmore
Letter to Millard Fillmore,
January 19, 1830.

On the theory that it never hurts a child to read something that may be above his head, and that books written down for children often do not awaken a dormant curiosity, this guidebook took its present form.

Jacqueline Kennedy
Foreword to the guidebook, *The White House: An Historic Guide*, which Mrs. Kennedy proposed and helped prepare. First planned as a guidebook for children, the finished book, aimed for adults and scholars, included a history of the White House and its architectural significance. Richly illustrated, the book was published in July 1963 by the White House Historical Association.

Ronald Reagan

. . . he is my hero.

Nancy Reagan
Look, October 31, 1967.

If you're taking a poll, you can put me in Ronald Reagan's column.

Nancy Reagan
Comments to reporters, Atlanta,
Georgia, October 10, 1984.

Regrets

I think people who tell you they have regrets are dumb.

Barbara Bush
Telling reporters that she has no
regrets about dropping out of college
in 1945 to marry George Bush. Press
conference, Washington, D.C.,
January 14, 1989.

Relationship

. . . hospitable intercourse . . . form the best trait in the character of
any place.

Dolley Madison
Letter to Eliza Collins Lee, 1803.

The perfect relationship is that one where two people do not even
need to tell each other how they feel or what they want, but care so
much for each other that one look and the sound of a voice will tell
them what is needed for happiness and calmness in the household.

Eleanor Roosevelt
Radio address, December 30, 1932.

Relaxing

Just sitting [on the beach] with the glorious rhythm of the waves coming in can be the most relaxing thing in the world, or watching the children build sand castles, and the excitement of finding rare sea shells . . .

Claudia Lady Bird Johnson
Interview, *U.S. News & World Report*,
February 22, 1965.

Religion

In vain have I summoned philosophy, its aid in vain. Come then Religion thy force can alone support the mind under the severest trials and hardest conflicts human nature is subject to.

Abigail Adams
Letter to John Thaxter,
February 15, 1778.

. . . my religion sanctions it, and I prefer my duty to God, to my duty to man.

Louisa Adams
Letter to President James Monroe,
August 17, 1818, seeking aid and
compassion for her sister, whose husband had resigned from government
service through pique.

I'm blessed with the kind of religious faith and upbringing that has given me a lot that I can fall back on.

Hillary Rodham Clinton
On *Live With Regis & Kathie Lee*, ABC,
June 10, 1996.

True religion is no more and no less than the relationship between man and his God.

Grace Coolidge
Letter to her son John Coolidge,
November 7, 1948.

The state of religion is quite low in this place.

Anna Harrison
Letter to Phoebe R. Reese,
November 12, 1834.

For your Mother's sake don't neglect church and . . . don't speak slightingly of religion.

Lucy Hayes
Letter to Scott Hayes,
November 17, 1888.

If we are to live successfully in this world we must make religion a vital thing, not theory but mode of living, way of life.

Eleanor Roosevelt
Address to Chautauqua Women's
Club, Chautauqua, New York,
July 25, 1933.

I believe there should be freedom for every child to be educated in his own religion. In public schools it should be taught that the spiritual side of life is most important. I would be happy if some agreement could be reached on passages from the Bible and some prayer that could be used. The real religious teaching of any child must be done by his own church and in his own home.

Eleanor Roosevelt
Letter to Cardinal Francis Spellman,
July 23, 1949.

Remarks

I got away with murder [as Second Lady]. I'm now slightly more careful about what I say. Slightly.

Barbara Bush
Quoted, "The Silver Fox," by
Michael Duffy, *Time*,
January 23, 1989.

Republican

I never failed to urge my husband to be an extreme Republican.

Mary Lincoln
Letter to Elizabeth Keckley,
October 29, 1867.

Respect

Freedom and respect are not values that should be in conflict with each other. They are basic American values that reinforce each other. But we cannot debate our differences nor face our mutual challenge unless and until we respect each other, men and women, young and old, across the ethnic and racial lines that divide each.

Hillary Rodham Clinton
Commencement address, University
of Pennsylvania, May 17, 1993.

If I could not have both I should choose my children's respect rather than their love.

Edith Kermit Roosevelt
Letter to Ethel Roosevelt Derby,
September 22, 1927.

Responsibility

I believe that personal reponsibility is at the root of any kind of social structure, including family.

Hillary Rodham Clinton
Quoted by Dotson Rader in "We Are
All Responsible," *Parade*,
April 11, 1993.

I think that every little child should have to learn how to tie his or her own shoelace.

> **Hillary Rodham Clinton**
> Quoted by Diane Loomans, *Body Mind Spirit*,
> October-November 1995.

A lot of the responsibility falls on the people left behind.

> **Hillary Rodham Clinton**
> Referring to families left behind by U.S. troops ordered to Bosnia. Statement made when opening the White House holiday season, December 4, 1995.

. . . responsibility is spread all the way across society.

> **Hillary Rodham Clinton**
> Quoted in *Newsweek*,
> January 15, 1996.

Each of us is responsible for ourselves.

> **Betty Ford**
> Quoted by Pamela Warrick, *Los Angeles Times*, November 12, 1995.

. . . the bearing of responsibility in maturity is much easier if one has grown gradually into the consciousness of it and has had experience in execution of smaller responsibilities.

> **Lou Henry Hoover**
> Radio speech, *NBC*, to 4-H Boys and Girls Clubs, June 22, 1929.

All these new duties and responsibilities it is "up to me" as the boys say to fulfill to the best of my ability, & I must "brook no continuance of weakmindedness."

> **Ellen Axson Wilson**
> Letter, June 28, 1902, to Miss Florence Hoyt, explaining how she dreaded the new duties that she would have to assume when her husband became president of Princeton University.

Retirement

I have lived long enough, and seen enough of the world, to check expectations, and to bring my mind to my circumstances, and retiring to our own little farm feeding our poultry and improving my garden has more charms for my fancy, than residing at the court of Saint James's where I seldom meet with characters so inoffensive as my Hens and chickens, or minds so well improved as my garden.

Abigail Adams
Letter to Thomas Jefferson,
February 26, 1788.

Our desires are moderate, our economy strict, our income, though moderate, will furnish us with all the necessaries, and many of the comforts of Life.

Abigail Adams
Letter to Mary Cranch,
February 7, 1801.

Where I was bitter, he was tolerant; where I resented, he was amused; and by the time we reached the corner of Massachusetts Avenue where we turned into S Street we were both happy and felt a great burden had been lifted from our shoulders and that we could return to our own affairs in a home of peace and serenity.

Edith Wilson
Describing the relief of her husband Woodrow Wilson having turned the Presidency over to Warren G. Harding, March 4, 1921. *My Memoir*, 1939.

Edith Wilson

Rightness

We should all do something to right the wrongs we see and not just complain about them. We owe that to our country.

Jacqueline Kennedy
In a televised speech on behalf of the
John F. Kennedy Library,
May 29, 1964.

But if I didn't do what I think is the right thing to do, I wouldn't be satisfied with myself.

Eleanor Roosevelt
White House press conference,
May 5, 1933.

Rights

The basic rationale for depriving people of rights in a dependency relationship is that certain individuals are incapable or undeserving of the right to take care of themselves and consequently need social institutions specifically designed to safeguard their position. Along with family, past and present examples of such arrangements include marriage, slavery, and the Indian reservation system.

Hillary Rodham Clinton
"Children Under the Law: The Rights
of Children," *Harvard Educational
Review*, 1973.

Eleanor Roosevelt

I am a die-hard Eleanor Roosevelt fan. I have read her autobiography, her newspaper columns, and many books about her and President Roosevelt. And from the first time I can remember hearing about her, I have always admired her.

Hillary Rodham Clinton
Address at the dedication of the
Eleanor Roosevelt College,
January 26, 1995.

I am often challenged, as I ask myself, am I even living up to one small percentage of the example she set, because it was ground breaking. There will never be another woman who did what she did.

> **Hillary Rodham Clinton**
> Speaking of Eleanor Roosevelt, when she was presented with the Eleanor Roosevelt Val-Kill Medal in Hyde Park, New York, October 2, 1995.

Eleanor Roosevelt was another important role model for me. I admired her ability to speak out in support of her beliefs, although I didn't always agree with the causes she championed.

> **Betty Ford**
> *Betty: A Glad Awakening,*
> with Chris Chase, 1987.

Courage sustained by compassion—that was the watchword of her entire career.

> **Claudia Lady Bird Johnson**
> Speech, Eleanor Roosevelt Memorial Foundation first anniversary luncheon, New York, April 9, 1964.

. . . a truly great American lady who always seemed to be "larger than life" to me. . . . I didn't agree with everything she did, you couldn't help but be a fan. Whether you were a Republican or Democrat didn't make any difference.

> **Nancy Reagan**
> Remarks at White House luncheon honoring Eleanor Roosevelt on the centennial of her birth, October 9, 1984.

Franklin D. Roosevelt

As to public service, I am hopeful, for I believe Franklin is a shrewd statesman.

> **Edith Kermit Roosevelt**
> Letter to Arthur Lee, September 29, 1933, on the administration of President Franklin D. Roosevelt.

The Assistant Secretary of the Navy and Mrs. Franklin D. Roosevelt also came back with us, and we found them very delightful companions.

Edith Wilson
Describing shipboard companions when President Wilson returned from European peace talks in July 1919. *My Memoir*, 1939.

Theodore Roosevelt

. . . [my] oldest and rather worst child.

Edith Kermit Roosevelt
Referring to her boyish and playful husband; quoted by Nicholas Roosevelt in *TR: The Man As I Knew Him*, 1967.

. . . I am so boiling mad when I read the account of that villain's speech about you (I mean T.R.) at Plattsburg that I could hardly eat my breakfast. Did you stoop to read it?

Edith Wilson
Letter to Woodrow Wilson, August 26, 1915, venting her ire over former President Theodore Roosevelt's criticism of Wilson's policies.

Sacrifice

Though I have been called to sacrifice to my Country, I can glory in my sacrifice, and derive pleasure from my intimate connection with one who is estimeed worthy of the important trust devolved upon him.

Abigail Adams
Letter to John Adams, May 18, 1778.

Scouting

To me the outing part of Scouting has always been the most important.

> **Lou Henry Hoover**
> Comments at Girl Scouts National
> Convention, Savannah, Georgia,
> January 25, 1922.

Secrets

Why would he tell me any secrets when he says I begin every sentence with "Don't tell George [Bush] I told you this, but . . . "

> **Barbara Bush**
> Quoted in "The Silver Fox," by
> Michael Duffy, *Time*,
> January 23, 1989.

I can't keep a secret.

> **Barbara Bush**
> On her inability to keep secrets, saying that she and her husband both
> agreed that he shouldn't tell her one.
> *U.S. News & World Report*, May 28,
> 1990.

I don't tell everything.

> **Patricia Pat Nixon**
> *Time*, August 19, 1974.

Secret Service

The secret service men, like the poor, we had with us always [alluding to Matthew 26:11], but it never seemed to me that they "lived" anywhere. They were merely around all the time.

> **Helen Taft**
> *Recollections of Full Years*, 1914.

Their job is one of the most important in our country, because no matter who is the president or vice president that person stands for America. So in effect they are safeguarding our entire country, not just an individual or family.

> **Hillary Rodham Clinton**
> *ABC-TV Good Morning America,*
> December 23, 1997.

Self-Aggrandizing

I was raised not to talk about myself.

> **Hillary Rodham Clinton**
> *Newsweek,* January 15, 1996.

My husband placed great confidence in my knowledge of human nature. He had no knowledge of men.

> **Mary Lincoln**
> Quoted by William H. Herndon in
> "Mrs. Lincoln's Denial, and What
> She Says." January 12, 1874.

The rest of the family doesn't seem to suspect that I have "had more than is good for me," anymore than they suspect what an extraordinary woman I am—how very superior to the rest of my sex!

> **Ellen Axson Wilson**
> Letter to Woodrow Wilson,
> March 10, 1890.

Ellen Axson Wilson

Self-Control

. . . self-control . . . is a thing one can best achieve alone . . .

> **Ellen Axson Wilson**
> Letter to Florence S. Hoyt,
> May 22, 1905.

Self-Identity

Go flatter'd image tell the tale of years long past away;
Of faded youth, of sorrow wail, of times too sure decay . . .

> **Louisa Adams**
> "To My Sons with My Portrait by
> [Gilbert] Stuart,"
> December 18, 1825.

Self-Image

I think that when we meet you will cease to love me as I really am
not the Louisa you were acquainted with. I am so miserably dull, stu-
pid and wan that I have gained the appelation of the Nun . . .

> **Louisa Adams**
> Letter to John Quincy Adams,
> December 20, 1796.

At last I get a chance to prove that I'm more than just a pretty face.

> **Barbara Bush**
> Opening remarks at the Alfred E.
> Smith Memorial Dinner, New York,
> October 19, 1989.

I am not pure. I'm just normal.

> **Rosalynn Carter**
> Quoted, *The New York Times*,
> June 11, 1976.

I was raised to really believe that what was important was what you
thought about yourself and how you measured up to the standards
you set for yourself.

> **Hillary Rodham Clinton**
> News conference, White House,
> April 22, 1994.

I am surprised at the way people seem to perceive me, and sometimes I read stories and hear things about me and I go "ugh." I wouldn't like her either.

Hillary Rodham Clinton
White House luncheon for women
reporters, January 9, 1995.

I have let other people define me. The stories come and go; I remain the same.

Hillary Rodham Clinton
News conference,
February 17, 1995.

The truth of the matter is that I am a very shy person.

Jacqueline Kennedy Onassis
Interview, *Kaybam International*,
May 25, 1972.

Self-Interest

This is a selfish world you know. Interest governs it, there are but very few, who are moved by any other Spring. They are Generous, Benevolent and Friendly when it is for their interest, when any thing is to be got by it, but touch the tender part, their interest, and you will immediately find the reverse, the greater half the World are mere Januses.

Abigail Adams
Letter to Mary Cranch,
October 6, 1766.

Self-Pity

What a world of anguish this is—and how I have been made to suffer!

Mary Lincoln
Letter to Elizabeth Keckley,
October 8, 1867.

Sensibility

. . . women know not only what men know, but much that men will never know. For, how many men really know the heart and soul of a woman?

Eleanor Roosevelt
My Day, March 6, 1937.

Service

Service is not a one-way street. Service is not about doing something for somebody else and that's the end. Service is being committed and being a part of the community in which you live, and it means that you get as well as you give.

Hillary Rodham Clinton
Comments during a White House ceremony honoring local young leaders on National Youth Service Day, April 20, 1993.

Well, I am very happy, because over these past eight years in the White House, I have found how to serve. And for that I will be forever grateful to the American people.

Nancy Reagan
Address to members of a gas industry conference, Washington, D.C., June 9, 1988.

Sex Discrimination

Our sex are ever losers, when they stem the torrent of public opinion.

Dolley Madison
Letter to her niece Mary Cutts, December 1, 1834.

Sex, Premarital

Well, they are, aren't they?

Betty Ford
Responding to a question about
young people living together before
they are married. *60 Minutes, CBS*,
August 10, 1975.

William Shakespeare

Shakespeare says everything for me.

Edith Kermit Roosevelt
Undated letter to her son
Kermit Roosevelt.

Do you suppose Shakspere [sic] made his men such poor creatures as
a rule and his women such paragons!

Ellen Axson Wilson
Letter to Woodrow Wilson,
March 22, 1885.

Shallowness

A person would be a fool to let his head be turned by externals, they
simply go with the position.

Ellen Axson Wilson
Comments to Florence S. Hoyt, circa
March 1913, on her noninterest in
setting fashion trends as the First Lady.

Shoes

I am perfectly comfortable in high heels. It is a matter of pride.

Patricia Pat Nixon
News conference, San Francisco,
August 20, 1956.

Shopping

. . . although my conscience hurts me dreadfully [over spending $475 on a coat] and I want to come and sit in your lap and have you tell me you love me even if I am extravagant . . . .

Edith Wilson
Letter to Woodrow Wilson,
November 30, 1915.

Sightseeing

You know I am so fond of sight-seeing.

Mary Lincoln
Letter to Abraham Lincoln,
May 1848.

Silence

I must impose a silence upon myself when I long to talk.

Abigail Adams
Letter to John Adams,
February 20, 1796.

. . . [I] am learning to hold my tongue well.

Dolley Madison
Letter to Anna Payne, May 22, 1804.

I know a lot but you have to keep it to yourself when you're in this position.

Patricia Pat Nixon
Ladies Home Journal,
February 1972.

Singing

We are out of doors most of the time, walking together and reading, unless I coerce him into singing, for he has a beautiful voice.

Ellen Axson Wilson
Letter to Mary W. Hoyt, cousin of Woodrow Wilson, describing her honeymoon in the hills of North Carolina, June–July 1885.

Single-Minded

I am altogether too one-idead [sic], and it is a terrible quality for a woman.

Ellen Axson Wilson
Letter to Woodrow Wilson, March 28, 1885.

Slavery

I wish most sincerely there was not a slave in the province. It always appeared a most iniquitious Scheme to me—fight ourselves for what we are daily robbing and plundering from those who have as good a right to freedom as we have.

Abigail Adams
Letter to John Adams, September 22, 1774.

Sleep

There is an inimitable, deep refreshment in sleeping out of doors.

Lou Henry Hoover
Radio address, NBC, to 4-H Boys and Girls Clubs, June 22, 1929.

Smile

A smile is necessary in this job [First Lady].

> **Mamie Eisenhower**
> Letter to Louise Caffey,
> June 10, 1953.

They told me in Washington that my husband should be able to get anything he wants with that smile of his.

> **Florence Harding**
> Comments to reporters covering the
> Republican National Convention,
> Chicago, June 12, 1920.

I think the qualities of gaiety, of joy, of happiness are especially meant to be found in women. These qualities are like smiles—they satisfy both those who wear them and those who see them.

> **Claudia Lady Bird Johnson**
> Remarks at the Congressional Prayer
> Breakfast, Washington, D.C.,
> February 1, 1967.

Smoking

I think that cigarette smoking is as addictive as drugs or alcohol.

> **Nancy Reagan**
> Press conference, White House,
> January 15, 1989.

Snoopers

Snoopers are born not made.

> **Edith Kermit Roosevelt**
> On the art of tracking down antique
> bargains in thrift stores; quoted by
> Archibald W. Butt in *Letters*, 1924.

Snub

I have no disposition to seclude myself from society, because I have met with unkind or ungrateful returns from some; I would strive to act my part well and Retire with that dignity which is unconscious of doing or wishing ill to any, with a temper disposed to forgive injuries, as I would myself hope to be forgiven, if any I have committed.

Abigail Adams
Letter to her sister, January 15, 1801.

A snub is the effort of a person who feels superior to make some one else feel inferior; to do so, he has to find some one who can be made to feel inferior.

Eleanor Roosevelt
White House press conference,
March 25, 1935.

Social Security

I hope very much to see a security program launched on its way which will include old age pensions, a permanent ban on child labor, better unemployment insurance, better health insurance for the country as a whole, better care for mothers and children generally.

Eleanor Roosevelt
White House press conference,
February 27, 1935.

Society

Civil society is the vehicle for our values, the way we convey who we are and what we stand for. When we encounter the inevitable setbacks and historical bumps in the road, the alliance of values that fuels civil society is what will carry us through.

Hillary Rodham Clinton
Speech, Prague, Czech Republic,
July 4, 1996.

An America that achieves as a great society can be a model to the world—a translation of American ideals into opportunity.

> **Claudia Lady Bird Johnson**
> Speech at luncheon by the Federated
> Democratic Women of Ohio,
> Columbus, Ohio,
> September 18, 1964.

. . . an impersonal government can't change society. There are good programs on the books, but it takes people to change society.

> **Patricia Pat Nixon**
> News conference, Springfield,
> Missouri, March 6, 1970.

A society in which everyone works is not necessarily a free society and may indeed be a slave society; on the other hand, a society in which there is widespread economic insecurity can turn freedom into a barren and vapid right for millions of people.

> **Eleanor Roosevelt**
> United Nations speech, Paris,
> September 27, 1948.

Speech, Freedom of

As women are not masons, or bound to keep secrets, they are entitled to a greater latitude of speech than Men.

> **Abigail Adams**
> Letter to William Shaw,
> December 21, 1798.

Stamina

I've never tired. I am never afraid. I don't get ill.

> **Patricia Pat Nixon**
> Quoted by Jessamyn West, "The Real
> Pat Nixon: An Intimate View," *Good
> Housekeeping*, February 1971.

Standards

. . . I was raised to really believe that what was important was what you thought about yourself and how you measured up to the standards you set for yourself. And I think, if my father and mother said anything to me more than a million times, it was, "Don't listen to what other people say, don't be guided by other people's opinions; you know, you have to live with yourself." And I think that's good advice. I mean, I'm glad I got it as a girl growing up, and I've passed it on to my daughter.

Hillary Rodham Clinton
Press conference, White House,
April 22, 1994.

Stereotypes

If you're under twenty-five, you're an apathetic Generation X-er. If you're over forty, you're a self-indulgent baby boomer. If you're a liberal, you're a bleeding heart, and if you're a conservative, you have no heart. And if you're the current sitting president, you're all of the above, depending on what day it is. And if you're the wife of the current sitting president, well, you just better make sure your hair is in place.

Hillary Rodham Clinton
Urging graduates to shun stereotypes,
commencement address, University
of Maryland, College Park, Maryland,
May 24, 1996.

Success

Success has many faces; it need not be circumscribed by a title, a job, a cause. Success is not always "getting." It is more often "giving." It does not consist of what we do, but rather of what we are. Success is not always an accomplishment. It can be a state of mind. The quiet dignity of a home, the relationship of the individuals in that home. The continuing expression of an inquiring mind can mean more in terms of success than all the surface symbols of status.

Claudia Lady Bird Johnson
Speech, Georgetown Visitation
Preparatory School, Washington, D.C.,
June 1, 1964.

Sufferings

Desire and Sorrow were denounced upon our Sex; as a punishment for the transgression of Eve. I have sometimes thought we are formed to experience more exquisite Sensations than is the Lot of your Sex. More tender and susceptable by Nature of those impression[s] which create happiness or misiry [sic], we Suffer and enjoy in a higher degree.

Abigail Adams
Letter to John Adams,
April 10, 1782.

Suffrage

. . . [I] never thought women were downtrodden by the men before they had the vote.

Lou Henry Hoover
New York Journal, June 15, 1928.

The whole point in women's suffrage is that the government needs the point of view of all its citizens and the women have a point of view which is of value to the government. If they have not, then there is no excuse and no answer to the arguments against woman suffrage.

Eleanor Roosevelt
Speech, state convention of the New York Democratic Party, Albany, New York, April 14, 1924.

Surfing

Surf-riding at Waikiki Beach is a great game. . . . when you see a beautiful, slim, brown native, naked save for short swimming trunks, come gliding down a high white breaker, poised like Mercury, erect on a single narrow plank—it looks delightfully exhilarating.

Helen Taft
Reflections of Full Years, 1914.

Sympathy

. . . the silent sympathy of Friends who have felt the like dispensation speaks a language better known to the heart than the most expressive eloquence can communicate.

Martha Washington
Letter to Janet Livingston Montgomery, April 5, 1800.

Talking

. . . I love talking about myself . . . (laughing)

Barbara Bush
Former First Ladies Forum, Kennedy Center, Washington, D.C., March 9, 1998.

One of the things I like most about all the parties we've had is that everybody talks.

> **Hillary Rodham Clinton**
> Interview, *The Washington Post*,
> November 24, 1993.

. . . it's a constant effort to keep talking to each other about how we can get along better.

> **Hillary Rodham Clinton**
> Comments at youth rally sponsored
> by Team Harmony, Boston,
> Massachusetts, December 9, 1997.

Sometimes I wonder if Mr. Coolidge would have talked with me more freely if I had been of a more serious turn of mind.

> **Grace Coolidge**
> "A Wife Remembers," *Meet Calvin
> Coolidge*,1960.

I leave all the talking to Ike.

> **Mamie Eisenhower**
> *Boston Herald*, November 4, 1952.

I do not believe that being First Lady should prevent me from expressing my views . . . Why should my husband's job or yours prevent us from being ourselves? Being ladylike does not require silence.

> **Betty Ford**
> Speech, Greater Cleveland
> International Woman's Year
> Congress, October 25, 1975.

Being able to talk nearly as much as I want to at home, I cannot express myself in a few words.

> **Lou Henry Hoover**
> Speech to Women's Branch of
> Hoover-for-President Engineers
> National Committee, New York,
> October 22, 1928.

We have to face the fact that either all of us are going to die together or we are going to learn to live together and if we are to live together we have to talk.

> **Eleanor Roosevelt**
> Quoted by David Gurewitsch, *The New York Times*, October 15, 1960.

Teaching

I think that to teach means to tell people something. I do not think it means to advocate something.

> **Eleanor Roosevelt**
> White House press conference, November 16, 1935.

Tears

I crush back the tears just as long as I can for I know they make you unhappy.

> **Lucretia Garfield**
> Letter to James A. Garfield, February 3, 1860, when she became discouraged by his coolness toward their marriage.

My tears blind me.

> **Julia Dent Grant**
> Letter to Mrs. William S. Hillyer, the wife of a former Army officer, informing her of President Grant's illness, 1885.

Telephone

When I die I'm going to have a phone in one hand and my phone book in the other.

Nancy Reagan
On her frequent use of the telephone; press conference, White House, January 15, 1989.

Television

I am so convinced that what people see on television absolutely affects how they treat children and how they feel about themselves. I am tired of folks saying we can't change television because that's censorship. . . . We ought to start by saying we're going to change what we see and how we treat each other.

Hillary Rodham Clinton
Decrying violence on television; "The Oprah Winfrey Show," *ABC*, May 16, 1995.

I think TV has completely revolutionized what should go on at a political convention. I was bored to death by the parades and floor demonstrations. If we can possibly prevent any such goings-on at our convention, it would gain in dignity and interest and in educational value to the TV audience.

Eleanor Roosevelt
Letter to Democratic National Chairman Frank E. McKinney, July 13, 1952.

Temperance

When it is legal to serve beer in any government house, it will naturally be proper to do so for any one who desires it at the White House. . . . I myself do not drink anything with alcoholic content, but that is purely as an individual thing. I should not dream of imposing my own convictions on other people as long as they live up to the law of our land.

Eleanor Roosevelt
Press conference, White House,
April 3, 1933.

Thanksgiving

Thanksgiving offers all of us the opportunity to reflect upon the positive aspect of our lives.

Patricia Pat Nixon
Thanksgiving Day message,
November 23, 1970.

Tolerance

One of the trends that I find very troubling is the increasing inequality that exists, not only between income groups that has been exacerbated over the last several years, but the attitudes that go along with that income inequality.

Hillary Rodham Clinton
Speech, Greater Detroit Chamber of
Commerce, June 1, 1995.

There are a lot of people I don't like, but I try—I try to remember to respect everybody and to see in everybody's story something that I can learn from.

Hillary Rodham Clinton
Comments at youth rally sponsored
by Team Harmony, Boston,
Massachusetts, December 9, 1997.

We should really try to stand always with the people who are trying to be tolerant and to act justly . . . and to strive to . . . keep from judging other people harshly when they do not always achieve our ideal.

> **Eleanor Roosevelt**
> Address to the luncheon of the
> Washington Round Table of the
> National Conference of Christians
> and Jews, April 13, 1939.

Tomorrow

Lyndon [Johnson] acts like there was never going to be a tomorrow.

> **Claudia Lady Bird Johnson**
> *The New York Times Magazine*,
> November 14, 1964.

Tone-Deaf

I was very surprised. I didn't know they gave Grammys to tone-deaf people like me.

> **Hillary Rodham Clinton**
> Comments to reporters upon receiving a Grammy award for the best spoken or non-musical album. The award was for the audio version of her book, *It Takes a Village*, New York, February 26, 1997.

Tranquility

I was born with a peace of mind. It is a matter of inheritance, training and experience.

> **Grace Coolidge**
> Speaking to a reporter about herself, 1946.

Traveler

. . . had nature formed me of the other Sex, I should certainly have been a rover.

Abigail Adams
Letter to Isaac Smith, Jr.,
April 20, 1771.

Harry S. Truman

. . . the loneliest man I ever saw. . . . I am sorry for him & he tries so hard.

Eleanor Roosevelt
Letter to Lorena Hickok, June 11,
1945, describing her visit with
President Truman.

Harry and Bess Truman

When you think of the Trumans, you think of the *best of this country*—its strong fiber, its courage, its resolve, and its patriotism.

Claudia Lady Bird Johnson
Remarks at the presentation of the
portrait of Bess Truman to the White
House, April 18, 1968.

Harry and I have been sweethearts and married more than forty years—and no matter where I was, when I put out my hand Harry's was there to grasp it.

Bess Truman
Reply when asked by an old friend
what she considered the most mem-
orable aspect of her life. Marianne
Means, *The Woman in the
White House*, 1963.

Trust

I think every person, man or woman, needs someone who is a safe person to talk to. In order to get that trust, you have to be safe, and I think I was that for George Bush.

> **Barbara Bush**
> Quoted by Henry Louis Gates, Jr.,
> *The New Yorker*, Combined Issue of
> February 26 and March 4, 1996.

Truth

It may be more important to see clearly, to reason honestly, to report accurately, to try and see and speak and to live the truth—in our work and play—that is about as much as we can aspire to do in our affairs in this world.

> **Lou Henry Hoover**
> Radio address, *NBC*, to 4-H Boys
> and Girls Clubs, June 22, 1929.

Is it any danger from telling the truth as you see it? I didn't think so. And so I did it.

> **Claudia Lady Bird Johnson**
> Interview with Ted Koppel, *Nightline*
> *ABC-TV*, October 8, 1997. Koppel
> had asked her about the value and
> danger of public people keeping
> diaries. Mrs. Johnson recorded her
> diary while in the White House.

Mark Twain

His strength was his simplicity. He told the story of the adventuring American children and a river, and with it, he produced an honest description about the pain and the glory of being alive as an American child.

> **Claudia Lady Bird Johnson**
> Remarks at the home of Mark Twain,
> Hannibal, Missouri,
> September 21, 1967.

Ugliness

Ugliness is bitterness.

Claudia Lady Bird Johnson
White House Conference on Natural
Beauty, May 24, 1965.

Understanding

Franklin [Roosevelt] had a good way of simplifying things. He made people feel that he had a real understanding of things and they felt they had about the same understanding.

Eleanor Roosevelt
Newspaper *PM*, April 6, 1947.

United Nations

We would remember that the United Nations is not a cure-all. It is only an instrument capable of effective action when its members have a will to make it work.

Eleanor Roosevelt
Speech, Democratic National
Convention, Chicago, July 22, 1952.

Values

Women who pack lunch for their kids, or take the early bus to work, or stay out late at the PTA or spend every spare minute tending to aging parents don't need lectures from Washington about values . . . . They, and us, need understanding and a helping hand to solve our own problems.

Hillary Rodham Clinton
Commencement address, Wellesley College, Wellesley, Massachusetts, May 29, 1992.

Vanity

My heart never yielded to worldly honors or self-vanity.

Sarah Childress Polk
Quoted in Anson and Fanny Nelson, *Memorials of Sarah Childress Polk*, 1892.

Vietnam War

This country needs to be united. And sadly, sadly, he [Lyndon B. Johnson] wasn't the man who could do it.

Claudia Lady Bird Johnson
On President Johnson's decision not to seek reelection, *The Washington Post*, March 23, 1995.

Virtues

We must press on that intricate path leading to perfection and happiness, by doing all that is good and noble, before we can be taken under the silver wing of our rewarding angel; this I feel sure you will aim at, and succeed beyond doubt. It will not be necessary, dear child, to recapitulate all the virtues important to render us worthy and deserving of good fortune, because you know them well.

Dolley Madison

Dolley Madison
Letter to her sister, Mary Payne Cutts, August 1, 1833.

Vision

. . . men who lack vision are poor in hope.

Eleanor Roosevelt
Speech, Democratic National Convention, Chicago, July 22, 1952.

Visits

Oh these visits make me sick many times, and I really sometimes think they will make me crazy.

Louisa Adams
Comments on her visits with the wives of Washington political notables; diary entry, date uncertain.

Volunteerism

. . . plan how you may help those who want desperately to help themselves, but can find no practical way to do so.

Lou Henry Hoover
Radio broadcast to 4-H Clubs,
November 7, 1931.

I am going to have lots of projects. I'm just a doer. I like to be busy and help out.

Patricia Pat Nixon
Quoted, *The New York Times*,
January 26, 1970.

Our success as a nation depends upon our willingness to give generously of ourselves for the welfare and enrichment of the lives of others.

Patricia Pat Nixon
Press luncheon, February 18, 1970.

Voting

Women do have the right to vote but unfortunately, many women in our country today do not exercise that vote.

Hillary Rodham Clinton
Remarks on celebrating the 75th
anniversary of the ratification of the
19th Amendment to the U.S.
Constitution, Grand Teton National
Park, Wyoming, August 25, 1995.

I cast only one vote—for Jack. It is a rare thing to be able to vote for one's husband for President and I didn't want to dilute it by voting for anyone else.

Jacqueline Kennedy
Remark after the 1960 presidential
election; quoted by Arthur M.
Schlesinger, Jr.,
A Thousand Days, 1965.

People in my own family told me I should vote [in the 1964 presidential election]. I said, "I'm not going to vote." This is very emotional, . . . You see, I'd never voted until I was married to Jack. . . . Then this vote would have—he would have been alive for that vote. And I thought, "I'm not going to vote for any [other person], because this vote would have been his."

> **Jacqueline Kennedy Onassis**
> Oral history interview, New York,
> January 11, 1974.

Walking

Let's try walking for a change.

> **Rosalynn Carter**
> Her formula for coping with gasoline
> shortage; comments made during a
> visit to Springfield, Massachusetts,
> March 19, 1979.

War

It's sad. I mean, war is not nice.

> **Barbara Bush**
> Comments, referring to the Persian
> Gulf War, at a White House
> reception, January 23, 1991.

How incredible it all seems . . . it will be a long hard conflict which will call for the utmost effort by every one of us but we cannot doubt that the forces which have truth and right and justice on their side will win.

> **Grace Coolidge**
> Round robin letter to her friends,
> December 12, 1941.

The danger which troubled my husband was that war might be started not so much by big men as by the little ones. While big men know the needs for self-control and restraint—little men are sometimes moved more by fear and pride. If only in the future the big men can continue to make the little ones sit down and talk, before they start to fight.

Jacqueline Kennedy
Letter to Nikita Khrushchev,
December 1, 1963.

I do not think I have been as alarmed before but I have become worried and since we always have to sit down together when war comes to an end, I think before we have a third World War, we should sit down together.

Eleanor Roosevelt
Letter to Harry S. Truman,
March 13, 1948.

I cannot believe that war is the best solution. No one won the last war, and no one will win the next war.

Eleanor Roosevelt
Letter to Harry S. Truman,
March 22, 1948.

Mr. [John Foster] Dulles has just frightened most of our allies to death with a statement that there is an art in actually threatening war and coming to the brink but retreating from the brink.

Eleanor Roosevelt
Letter to Gus Ranis,
January 23, 1956.

I doe, my dear sister, most religiously wish there was an end to the war, that we might have the pleasure of meeting again.

Martha Washington
Letter to Nancy Bassett,
August 20, 1776.

Washington, D.C.

. . . [a] scene of utter desolation. The roads are impassable.

Louisa Adams
Her first impression of the capital
city, in her diary, "The Adventures of
a Nobody."

As I think back now, I don't believe I ever heard anyone describe Washington as a real home town. Still, . . . It did not take long to find out that the heart of Washington beats just like the heart of any other village or town or metropolis. The city is alive. It was a wonderful home town. . . .

Rosalynn Carter
Remarks at a special session of the
District of Columbia Council,
December 9, 1980.

I love this city. I loved living here and being so close to the seat of power, being part of the political system.

Rosalynn Carter
Comments at book luncheon,
Washington, D.C., April 12, 1984.

Dear Washington, how I love you, with your beautiful, broad, generous streets and blue skies! The sun shines always there for me.

Julia Dent Grant
*The Personal Memoirs of
Julia Dent Grant,*1975.

I wonder if anyone enjoys the beauty of this city as much as I do?

Claudia Lady Bird Johnson
Letter to Brooke Astor, April l3,
1967.

The process of leaving Washington after thirty-four years is a little like drowning. All your past flashes before you. We shall always miss this town.

Claudia Lady Bird Johnson
Remarks at the Women's National
Press Club dinner, Washington, D.C.,
December 2, 1968.

I find Washington very much as I expected both in appearance and climate—as to the former, my expectations were not very highly raised, and the latter has realized the favorable impression I had of it.

Jane Pierce
Letter to her father-in-law, Benjamin Pierce, December 1834.

I am so glad, you sweet thing, that you are beginning to love Washington. Nearly half of my life has been spent there and, while I would follow you wherever you went, I would always be a little hurt if you hated Washington, and if you can love it because I do and because you found me there, it will make me proud and happy and I will do all I can to make it from now on seem really like home . . .

Edith Wilson
Letter to Woodrow Wilson, August 9, 1915.

George Washington

I was struck with General Washington, . . . Dignity with ease, and complacency, the Gentleman and Soldier look agreeably blended in him. Modesty marks every line and feature of his face.

Abigail Adams
Letter to John Adams, June 16, 1775.

Take his character all together and we shall not look upon his like again.

Abigail Adams
Letter to Thomas Boylston Adams, November 8, 1796.

If we look through the whole tenor of his life, history will not produce to us a parallel.

Abigail Adams
On the death of George Washington, letter to Mary Cranch, December 22, 1799.

Our kind friend, Mr. Carroll, has come to hasten my departure, and is in a very bad humor with me because I insist on waiting until the large picture of Gen. Washington is secured . . . I have ordered the frame to be broken and the canvas taken out; it is done, and the precious portrait placed in the hands of two gentlemen of New York, for safe keeping. And now, dear sister, I must leave this house . . .

> **Dolley Madison**
> Letter to her sister, Anna Payne Cutts, August 23, 1814. Written as British troops were approaching the President's House [White House].

Martha Washington

She is plain in her dress, but that plainness is the best of every article. . . . Her manners are modest and unassuming, dignified and femenine, not the Tincture of ha'ture about her.

> **Abigail Adams**
> Letter to Mary Cranch, June 29, 1789.

Mrs. Washington is one of those unassuming characters which create love and esteem. A most becoming pleasantness sits upon her countenance and an unaffected deportment which renders her the object of veneration and respect.

> **Abigail Adams**
> Letter to Mary Cranch, July 12, 1789.

Wealth

. . . I know it is hard to read about people who are rich when you are not, and I do not want you to think us spoiled and heartless.

Jacqueline Kennedy
Letter to Ronald C. Munro of Birmingham, England, postmarked January 10, 1955. Munro had asked her to send him $20,000. While rejecting his plea, Mrs. Kennedy conceded that her husband was "well off," but after taxes and expenses, "there is not just a great pile of money lying around . . ."

Welfare

. . . take concern for the welfare of others' lives . . .

Lou Henry Hoover
Radio address on the welfare of children, *NBC*, March 7, 1931.

White House

You must keep all this to yourself, and, when asked how I like it, say that I write you the situation is beautiful, which is true. The house is made habitable, but there is not a single apartment finished . . . . This is a beautiful spot, capable of every improvement, and, the more I view it, the more I am delighted with it.

Abigail Adams
Letter to her daughter Abigail Adams Smith, November 21, 1800. John and Abigail Adams were the first occupants of the White House, then called the President's House.

... this House is built for ages to come.

Abigail Adams
Letter to her sister Mary Cranch,
November 21, 1800.

The President's House is in a beautiful situation in front of which is the Potomac with a view of Alexandria. The country around is romantic but a wild, a wilderness at present. ... [later, describing the living condition in her new home] I had much rather live in the house in Philadelphia. Not one room or chamber is finished of the whole. It is habitable by fires in every room, thirteen of which we are obliged to keep daily, or sleep in wet & damp places.

Abigail Adams
Upon her arrival in Washington,
letter to her sister Mary Cranch,
November 21, 1800.

There is something in this great unsocial house which depresses my spirits beyond expression and makes it impossible for me to feel at home or to fancy that I have a home any where.

Louisa Adams
Letter to her son, George
Washington Adams,
November 6, 1825.

Life inside the White House was great and believe it or not, it's great outside, too.

Barbara Bush
Remarks to Betty Boyd Caroli,
September 23, 1993.

I loved being in the White House. I felt as if I could do something for people.

Rosalynn Carter
Comments at New York luncheon,
June 13, 1983.

I am not saddened by the thought of leaving the White House.

Frances Cleveland
The New York Times, March 4, 1889.

We are coming back just four years from today.

Frances Cleveland
Remarks to the White House staff,
March 4, 1889.

That one floor had the smell of an old house by the sea, a musty
scent, overlaid with roses.

Frances Cleveland
Reply to her daughter, Esther, who
asked her mother if she remembered
anything curious about the smell of
the upstairs of the White House.
"Memories," *The New Yorker,*
January 27, 1962.

We love the second floor of the White House. We are left totally
alone. We don't have the Secret Service people following us and we
can tell the staff we will take care of ourselves, so it's like being in
your own house when you are up there.

Hillary Rodham Clinton
Quoted, *House Beautiful,*
March 1994.

I have gotten a little frustrated and itchy in the White House because
I feel cut off from people.

Hillary Rodham Clinton
Comments on the role of the First
Lady, George Washington University,
Washington, D.C.,
November 29, 1994.

There is no way in the world to figure out what it is like to live here.
There is so much about it no one ever tells you about. There are little
things you never would have thought of. You have to start thinking
about Christmas in April.

Hillary Rodham Clinton
White House luncheon for women
reporters, January 9, 1995.

We've actually had more family time together because, as I've told my friends, the President kind of lives above the store, and we manage to have dinner together practically every night.

Hillary Rodham Clinton
Quoted by Peter Maas, *Parade*,
February 19, 1995.

It would be a very lonely place to live, the White House, if the President couldn't invite people he wanted to know, or to see, to spend time with.

Hillary Rodham Clinton
Commenting on the impression that the White House was for sale by inviting political donors to spend the night there. Interview, *CNN* "Q & A,"
April 10, 1997.

I don't know what they expect me to do. Hang my wash in the East Room, like Abigail Adams?

Grace Coolidge
Comments to a friend before moving into the White House.

It was hard to leave our old friends in Washington, . . . It was a great lark, but a great responsibility. It is too bad that more women cannot have the opportunity of living in the White House. It is a great opportunity for service.

Grace Coolidge
Comments to newspaper reporters after returning to her home in Northampton, Massachusetts,
March 6, 1929.

The White House takes quite a bit of housekeeping.

Mamie Eisenhower
Letter to Maude Hurd,
August 7, 1953.

At times it is lonely and you can feel isolated.

Betty Ford
On living in the White House, news conference, August 4, 1975.

I enjoyed living there as I realized the history of the house and the few people who have lived there and what a special privilege it is.

Betty Ford
Interview, *The New York Times*,
January 25, 1977.

Eight happy years I spent there—so happy! It still seems as much like home to me as the old farm in Missouri, White Haven.

Julia Dent Grant
The Personal Memoirs of Julia Dent Grant, 1975.

The only reason I want to go to the White House is because it is his wish.

Florence Harding
Comments to reporters at the Republican nominating convention, Chicago, June 10, 1920.

Let 'em look if they want to! It's their White House.

Florence Harding
Orders to White House servants who were pulling down the window shades to keep people from peeking in on the reception following her husband's inauguration in March 1921.

Very few people understand to what straits the President's family has been put at times for lack of accommodations. Really, there are only five sleeping apartments and there is no feeling of privacy.

Caroline Harrison
Quoted in Esther Singleton, *The Story of the White House*, 2 vols., New York, 1907.

I think it is beautiful . . . I love this house for the associations that no other could have.

Lucy Hayes
Quoted by Miss Grundy, columnist, *Boston Herald*, March 28, 1878.

. . . I grew to love the house.

> **Lucy Hayes**
> On leaving the White House, letter
> to Lizzie Mills, spring, 1881.

I would rather be a doorkeeper in the house of God than to live in that palace [White House].

> **Rachel Jackson**
> Remarks to her maid Hannah, shortly
> before she collapsed and died,
> December 22, 1828; recalled by
> attending physician,
> Dr. Henry Lee Heiskell.

The first week I sort of tiptoed through the house.

> **Claudia Lady Bird Johnson**
> Describing her awe at living in the
> White House while taking news
> reporters on a tour of the White
> House living quarters,
> January 10, 1964.

Awareness of this house is like a shot of adrenalin—intensifying the desire to do the best you can to live up to what this country wants its first family to be.

> **Claudia Lady Bird Johnson**
> Interview, Associated Press,
> November 6, 1967.

It [Oval Room] is my favorite room in the White House—the one where I think the heart of the White House is—where the President receives all the Heads of State who visits him—where the honor guard is formed to march downstairs to "Hail to the Chief"—All ceremonies and all the private talks that really matters happens in that room—and it has the most beautiful proportions of any in the White House . . .

> **Jacqueline Kennedy**
> Letter to Mr. and Mrs. John Loeb,
> who contributed toward the White
> House restoration, 1961.

I just think that everything in the White House should be the best . . .

Jacqueline Kennedy
Comments to Charles Collingwood,
CBS, during televised tour of the
White House, February 14, 1962.

Don't be frightened of this house—some of the happiest years of my marriage have been spent here—you will be happy here.

Jacqueline Kennedy
To Claudia Lady Bird Johnson as she
prepared to leave the White House,
November 26, 1963.

I want to make the White House the first house in the land.

Jacqueline Kennedy
Quoted by Clark Clifford in *Counsel
to the President*, 1991.

Very different from home. We only have to give our orders for the dinner and dress in proper season.

Mary Lincoln
On dining in the White House, letter
to Hanna Shearer, August 1, 1861.

Our home is very beautiful, the grounds around us are enchanting . .

Mary Lincoln
Letter to Julia Ann Sprigg,
May 29, 1862.

I just couldn't go back to that place. Even driving around Washington I'd try to drive a way where I wouldn't see the White House.

Jacqueline Kennedy Onassis
On how she avoided the White
House after her husband had been
killed by an assassin; oral history
interview, New York,
January 11, 1974.

If I should be as fortunate as to reach the White House, I expect to live on $25,000 a year, and I will neither keep house nor make butter.

Sarah Childress Polk
Letter to a friend, 1844.

The White House was the abode of pleasure while I was there.

Sarah Childress Polk
Quoted in Anson and Fanny Nelson, *Memorials of Sarah Childress Polk*, 1892.

I don't think there is any such thing as a real vacation [when living in the White House] because—well, there can't be. I mean you can't just turn it off; you can't shut down the world.

Nancy Reagan
Interview, Mike Douglas television show, 1981.

I think about the White House being a special place, and that it should be considered as such, and should always be treated as such.

Nancy Reagan
Quoted, *Parade*, November 8, 1981.

But nobody, *nobody* can prepare you for what it's like being in the White House. I certainly wasn't.

Nancy Reagan
Interview, *The Washington Post*, August 24, 1984.

I don't think anybody can ever imagine how much of a change it is until you're actually here. Nobody can ever prepare you for the scrutiny that you're under.

Nancy Reagan
On living in the White House, interview with the *Associated Press*, January 15, 1985.

You live a magnified life, which means the highs are higher, the lows are lower, with every move you make exaggerated by the tremendous scrutiny of the media. It's a high-wire existence, and I wouldn't trade the experience for even extra years added to my life.

Nancy Reagan
On the experience of living in the
White House; address to members of
a gas industry conference,
Washington, D.C., June 9, 1989.

If you need a plumber, you get a plumber.

Nancy Reagan
Remark on the benefits of living in
the White House; interview, *CBS,
The Phil Donahue Show*, 1990.

To me the shadow [of President McKinley's assassination] still hangs over the White House, and I am in constant fear about Theodore . . .

Edith Kermit Roosevelt
Letter to Emily Carrow,
September 29, 1901.

It is a great pleasure to have guests now that I can make them comfortable.

Edith Kermit Roosevelt
After restoration of the White House;
letter to "Aunt Lizzie" [her husband's
aunt, Mrs. James R. Roosevelt],
January 26, 1903.

I doubt if even I was entirely happy for there was always that anxiety about the President . . . I never realized what a strain I was under continuously until it was over.

Edith Kermit Roosevelt
Quoted by Archibald W. Butt in *Taft
and Roosevelt*, 1930.

No woman entering the White House, if she accepts the fact that it belongs to the people and, therefore, must be representative of whatever conditions the people are facing, can light-heartedly take up her residence here.

> **Eleanor Roosevelt**
> Interview upon entering the White House, *Associated Press*, March 4, 1933.

There is never a free evening.

> **Eleanor Roosevelt**
> On living in the White House, radio broadcast, *WJZ*, September 25, 1934.

Living in the White House with its opportunity of helping people and understanding problems should make you live better the rest of your life.

> **Eleanor Roosevelt**
> Talk at Sinai Temple, Chicago, November 17, 1936.

. . . though I was always conscious of the character which a century of history had impressed upon the White House, it came, nevertheless, to feel much like home as any house I have ever occupied.

> **Helen Taft**
> *Recollections of Full Years*, 1914.

I made very few changes, really. As a matter of fact no President's wife ever needs to unless she so desires, because the White House is a governmental institution thoroughly equipped and always in good running order.

> **Helen Taft**
> *Recollections of Full Years*, 1914.

Most definitely would not have.

> **Bess Truman**
> Written reply to reporters who asked, "If it had been left to your own free choice would you have gone into the White House in the first place?" White House, October 29, 1947.

I am naturally the most unambitious of women and life in the White House has no attractions for me! Quite the contrary in fact!

Ellen Axson Wilson
Letter to President William Howard Taft, January 10, 1913, thanking him for providing her with information that would ease her family's move to Washington.

Whitewater

I'm holding up fine except that it's lonely in the bunker.

Hillary Rodham Clinton
On investigation of Whitewater land sales, *USA Today*, March 21, 1994.

This is an investigation in search of a scandal.

Hillary Rodham Clinton
Interview, *Los Angeles Times*, January 17, 1996.

It's been a long day.

Hillary Rodham Clinton
Comments to reporters after testifying before a grand jury on Whitewater legal documents, Washington, D.C., January 26. 1996.

Widowhood

I never got used to him being gone. He was my husband. He was my whole life.

Mamie Eisenhower
Interview, *Philadelphia Inquirer*, July 1974.

I'm always turning down pages of books, and remembering little amusing parts of conversations and thinking that I must remember to tell him that, and then remembering that I won't.

Claudia Lady Bird Johnson
On missing her husband, news conference, Johnson City, Texas, May 1973.

. . . I never used it [the word 'widow'], nor do I think of myself as being alone because I have a lot of family.

Claudia Lady Bird Johnson
Interview, *The New York Times*, March 22, 1982.

I don't think there is any consolation. What was lost cannot be replaced.

Jacqueline Kennedy
An essay, "A Memoir," she wrote for *Look* magazine, published November 27, 1964.

I realize more and more that I am not company for anyone but I do not wish to forget my friends. I am more lonely every day I live.

Ida McKinley
Letter to Webb C. Hayes, December 10, 1905.

Can anyone understand how it is to have lived in the White House, and then, suddenly, to be living alone as the President's widow?

Jacqueline Kennedy Onassis
Quoted by Billy Baldwin. *McCall's*, December 1974

Wife

I am ready and willing to follow my husband whenever he chooses.

Abigail Adams
Letter to John Adams, April 26, 1797.

However brilliant a woman's talents may be, she ought never to shine at the expence of her Husband.

Abigail Adams
Letter to Mary Cranch,
December 4, 1799.

No man ever prospered in the world without the consent and cooperation of his wife.

Abigail Adams
Letter to Elizabeth Shaw Peabody,
June 1809.

I just have a good relationship with Jimmy. It's not a position of an adviser. I am a wife. I like to know what's happening . . .

Rosalynn Carter
Washington Star, July 26, 1979.

. . . I'm not anybody you talk to in the government. I'm your wife!

Rosalynn Carter
To President Carter when he rejected her plea for additional help by noting that, "Anybody you talk to in the government wants one more staff member." *First Lady from Plains*, 1984.

. . . who is closer to the President, who better has his ear, than his wife?

Rosalynn Carter
Commenting on the criticism she received when representing President Carter during a 1977 tour of Latin America. *First Lady from Plains*, 1984.

. . . being a wife is the best career that life has to offer a woman.

Mamie Eisenhower
"If I Were a Bride Today," *True Confessions*, November 1954.

I never pretended to be anything but Ike's wife.

Mamie Eisenhower
Quoted, Julie Nixon Eisenhower, *Special People*, 1977.

I enjoy being a wife and a mother and all those things.

Betty Ford
Quoted in Sheila Rabb Weidenfeld,
First Lady's Lady, 1979.

I am going to try harder than ever before to be the best little wife possible.

Lucretia Garfield
Letter to James A. Garfield,
March 18, 1860.

I, too, have been the wife of a great leader.

Julia Dent Grant
To Queen Victoria, during a visit at
Windsor Castle in June 1877. Ishbel
Ross, *The General's Wife*, 1959.

I was such an excessively indulged wife—my darling husband was so gentle and easy.

Mary Lincoln
Letter to Mary Harlan Lincoln,
November 1870.

I think the best thing I can do is to be a distraction.

Jacqueline Kennedy
Reflecting on her role as a U.S.
senator's wife. *New York Post*,
March 25, 1957.

My motivating force . . . is to be a good wife.

Jacqueline Kennedy
Quoted, *Boston Globe*,
January 15, 1961.

The President's wife should be just that—his wife.

Jacqueline Kennedy
To Bonnie Angelo, April 16, 1962.

I just want to go down in history as the wife of the President.

Patricia Pat Nixon
Interview, December 14, 1969.

As long as man has lived in groups, there's been the question of what to do about the boss's wife.

Nancy Reagan
Speech, annual Associated Press luncheon for the American Publishers Association, Washington, D.C., May 4, 1987.

Do your own thing. Just because you're married doesn't mean you've given up your rights to have an opinion.

Nancy Reagan
Quoted, *The New York Times*, January 15, 1989.

He [Franklin D. Roosevelt] might have been happier with a wife who was completely uncritical. That I was never able to be, and he had to find it in other people. Nevertheless, I think I sometimes acted as a spur, even though the spurring was not always wanted or welcome. I was one of those who served his purposes.

Eleanor Roosevelt
This I Remember, 1949.

Woodrow Wilson

The only fear Woodrow Wilson knew was the fear of God should he fail in his own duty.

Edith Wilson
My Memoir, 1939.

Always remember dear One that you are not very Strong your self but that by your example you make us So—and that any one who is with you as I have been absorbs all the wholesome things and become better from the inspiration.

Edith Wilson
Letter to Woodrow Wilson, June 5, 1920.

People are apt to say after meeting him that, strange as his face is, they were even more impressed with the sympathy and kindliness of expression of his eyes and his smile.

Ellen Axson Wilson
Describing her husband as requested by the *St. Louis Post-Dispatch*, July 28, 1912.

Woman/Women

We need to understand that there is no one formula for how women should lead their lives.

Hillary Rodham Clinton
Remarks to the United Nations Fourth World Conference on Women, Beijing, China, September 5, 1995.

. . . some women are a lot smarter than men . . .

Betty Ford
Quoted, *St. Louis Globe-Democrat*, September 20, 1974.

Woman's mind is as strong as man's . . . equal in all things and is superior in some.

Lucy Hayes
Quoted by Emily Apt Geer, "Lucy Webb Hayes and Her Influence Upon Her Era," *Hayes Historical Journal*, 1976.

When a girl arrives at the age of twenty-one, we want her to do things instead of just thinking, to realize the importance of political affairs and to have a well-balanced mind developed equally by an early education in citizenship, religion, home making and play.

Lou Henry Hoover
Speech, Girl Scout Mass Meeting, Milwaukee, Wisconsin, May 18, 1935.

You are sorely needed. Your voice, your vision, and your fervor are sorely needed to help make this a better land.

Claudia Lady Bird Johnson
Speech, Kentucky Federation of
Women's Clubs Annual Convention,
Lexington, Kentucky, May 21, 1964.

He [John F. Kennedy] said to me a long time ago that one woman is worth ten men. They have the idealism, they have the time to give, and they work without making demands.

Jacqueline Kennedy
Quoted, *The Washington Star*,
October 15, 1960.

I have great terror of strong minded Ladies, . . .

Mary Lincoln
Letter to James Gordon Bennett,
October 4, 1862.

There is a saying that a woman is like a teabag. You don't know her strengths until she is in hot water.

Nancy Reagan
News conference, Dallas, Texas,
February 17, 1982.

The time appeals most strongly to the manhood and the womanhood of America. To woman more than ever because to her has come the perfected opportunity to make her influence weighty in behalf of the nation . . .

Edith Kermit Roosevelt
Statement issued to *The Women-
Republican*, September 13, 1920.

Men are given to thinking in the large, but women remember all the little things.

Eleanor Roosevelt
Address before Town Hall public
forum, Washington, D.C.,
February 2, 1936.

Every woman wants to be the first to someone sometime in her life & the desire is the explanation for many strange things women do, if only men understood it!

Eleanor Roosevelt
Letter to Joseph P. Lash,
January 21, 1944.

I am a woman—and the thought that you have need of me is sweet.

Edith Wilson
Letter to Woodrow Wilson,
May 4, 1915.

Seriously, dear, I fear you would find it very unpleasant to serve, as it were, under a woman! It seems so unnatural, so jarring to one's sense of the fitness of things—so absurd too.

Ellen Axson Wilson
Letter to Woodrow Wilson,
November 28, 1884, when he was
considering a teaching position at the
newly established Bryn Mawr College
for women. She later consented to
his acceptance of the position.

This is certainly the women's century! They have taken possession of the earth!

Ellen Axson Wilson
Letter to Woodrow Wilson, April 24,
1904, commenting on the number of
women travelers.

Women's Choices

I think the important thing for women's lives today and for girls thinking about their own future is to work for the opportunity to make whatever choices are right for your life and not be constrained by what other people think you should do.

Hillary Rodham Clinton
Addressing Girl Scouts, Lebanon,
New Hampshire, January 25, 1996.

A liberated woman is one who feels confident in herself, and is happy in what she is doing. She is a person who has a sense of self. I think it all comes down to freedom of choice.

Betty Ford
The New York Times,
November 8, 1975.

While opportunities are open to women today, too many are available only to the lucky few.

Betty Ford
Speech, International Women's Year
Congress, Cleveland, 1975.

I don't mean that women shouldn't have interests outside the home. I think it's very important that they do. But now I think that women who choose not to have a career feel self-conscious about it, and I don't think that's right.

Nancy Reagan
Redbook, July 1981.

Women's Health

In too many places, the status of women's health is a picture of human suffering and pain. The faces in that picture are of girls and women who, for the grace of God or the accident of birth, could be us or one of our sisters, mothers or daughters.

Hillary Rodham Clinton
Speech, United Nations Fourth
World Conference on Women,
Beijing, China, September 5, 1995.

The part that women play in the world has been greatly changed even in my own generation. It has been broadened and enlarged, and we will be wise if we recognize that a larger consideration for the health and physical advancement of girls will better fit them for the role they must assume.

Florence Harding
Letter to the National Board of Camp
Fire Girls, New York,
November 26, 1921.

Women's Power

Since this Society has been organized and so much thought and reading directed to the early struggles of this country, it has been made plain that much of its success was due to the character of the women of that era. The unselfish part they acted constantly commends itself to our admiration and example.

Caroline Harrison
Speech before the first Continental
Congress of the Daughters of the
American Revolution (DAR),
Washington, D.C., February 22,
1892. National Society, Daughters of
the American Revolution,
Americana Collection.

Women's Rights

I long to hear that you have declared an independency—and by the way in the new Code of Laws which I suppose it will be necessary for you to make I desire you would Remember the Ladies, and be more generous and favourable to them than your ancestors. Do not put such unlimited power into the hands of Husbands. Remember all Men would be tyrants if they could. If perticular care and attention is not paid to the Ladies we are determined to foment a Rebellion, and will not hold ourselves bound by any Laws in which we have no choice, or Representation . . . That your Sex are Naturally Tyrannical is a Truth so thoroughly established as to admit of no dispute, but such of you as wish to be happy willingly give up the harsh title of Master for the more tender and endearing one of Friend. Why then, not put it out of the power of the vicious and the Lawless to use us with cruelty and indignity with impunity. Men of Sense in all Ages abhor those customs which treat us only as the vassals of your happiness.

Abigail Adams
Letter to John Adams,
March 31, 1776.

I can not say I think you very generous to the Ladies, for whilst you are proclaiming peace and good will to Men, Emancipating all Nations, you insist upon retaining an absolute power over Wives. But you must remember that Arbitrary power is like most other things which are very hard, very liable to be broken—and notwithstanding all your wise Laws and Maxims we have it in our power not only to free ourselves but to subdue our Masters, and without violence throw both your natural and legal authority at your feet.

Abigail Adams
Letter to John Adams, May 7, 1776.

I will never consent to have our sex considered . . . inferior . . . Let each planet shine in their own orbit. God and nature designed it so—if man is Lord, woman is Lordess—that is what I contend for.

Abigail Adams
Letter to Elizabeth Shaw Peabody,
July 19, 1799.

I never felt I needed to be liberated.

Rosalynn Carter
Quoted, *The New York Times*,
November 6, 1977.

If women and girls don't flourish, families won't flourish. And if families don't flourish, communities and nations won't flourish.

Hillary Rodham Clinton
Remarks celebrating the 75th
anniversary of the ratification of the
19th Amendment to the U.S.
Constitution, Grand Teton National
Park, Wyoming, August 26, 1995.

It is time for us to say here in Beijing, and the world to hear, that it is no longer acceptable to discuss women's rights as separate from human rights.

Hillary Rodham Clinton
Speech, United Nations Fourth
World Conference on Women,
Beijing, China, September 6, 1995.

Women need to have the right and the opportunity to make incomes, to help themselves and their families.

> **Hillary Rodham Clinton**
> Quoted by Diane Loomans, *Body Mind Spirit*,
> October-November 1995.

A democracy depends on the full integration of women into society, especially on seeing to it that they have equal access to the same tools of opportunity as man.

> **Hillary Rodham Clinton**
> News conference, Harare, Zimbawe,
> March 21, 1997.

I think it's time for women to step up and take their place.

> **Betty Ford**
> Comments to White House reporters, August 13, 1974.

I feel that the liberated woman is the woman who is happy doing what she's doing, whether it's a job or as a housewife, it doesn't make a bit of difference. Just so she, inwardly feels that she is happy and that she is liberated.

> **Betty Ford**
> Interview, *60 Minutes, CBS*,
> August 10, 1975.

. . . so what's all this about liberated women being career women? Anyone who feels good about what she's doing in the home should have the same sense of liberation.

> **Betty Ford**
> Speech, Homemaking and Identity Conference, September 26, 1975.

Women should get paid whatever a man would get paid for the same job. I think it comes down to ability.

> **Nancy Reagan**
> Quoted, *The New York Times Magazine*, October 26, 1980.

Work

I have always worked.

Rosalynn Carter
Interview, *U.S. News & World Report*, October 18, 1976.

I need not be the shrinking slave of toil, but its regal master, making whatever I do yield me its best fruits.

Lucretia Garfield
Letter to James A. Garfield, circa 1871.

I never had time to dream about being anyone else, I had to work.

Patricia Pat Nixon
Quoted in Gloria Steinem, *Outrageous Acts*, 1983.

What has been sad for many women of my generation is that they weren't supposed to work if they had families. There they were, with the highest education, and what were they to do when the children were grown—watch the raindrops coming down the windowpane? . . . Of course women should work if they want to. You have to be doing something you enjoy. . . .

Jacqueline Kennedy Onassis
Interview, *Ms.* Magazine, March 1979.

No man works harder in the fields than the farmer's wife in her home and on the farm.

Eleanor Roosevelt
Radio broadcast, NBC, September 4, 1934.

. . . most women do the work they do because they do it better than men.

Eleanor Roosevelt
Address before Town Hall public forum, Washington, D.C., February 3, 1936.

Women can do almost anything men can do if they are trained for it.

Eleanor Roosevelt
Address, Syracuse University,
Syracuse, New York,
January 5, 1943.

When you cease to make a contribution you begin to die. Therefore, I think it a necessity to be doing something which you feel is helpful in order to grow old gracefully and contentedly.

Eleanor Roosevelt
Letter to Mr. Horns, February 19,
1960, quoted in Joseph P. Lash,
Eleanor: The Years Alone, 1972.

Worry

I'm a worrier. I worry a lot.

Nancy Reagan
Press conference, White House,
January 15, 1989.

Worthiness

It's the darnest thing, and I think the ladies will agree, that the day before you are married to the president-elect nobody gives a darn what you say, and the day after he is the president-elect people think you are brilliant and your causes are very good.

Barbara Bush
Former First Ladies Forum, Kennedy
Center, Washington, D.C.,
March 9, 1998.

Barbara Bush

I assure you that I have no sense of being "an unworthy American mother." The final judgment, my dear Cardinal Spellman, of the worthiness of all human beings is in the hands of God.

Eleanor Roosevelt
Letter to Cardinal Frances Spellman, July 23, 1949. The Cardinal had earlier accused her of anti-Catholic bias and "discrimination unworthy of an American mother" for supporting an educational bill introduced in the House of Representatives.

Writing/Writers

I'd write a chapter and then pass it on to Jean Becker who did the fact-checking and the spelling. I'm not great at spelling. I have a little laptop, and I wrote it on that.

Barbara Bush
On writing her book, *Barbara Bush: A Memoir*, quoted, *Parade*, September 25, 1994.

One thing about being shut up in that room. If I was writing about things that were really painful, I could cry. Nobody knew it. I could laugh out loud sometimes. I could be amazed sometimes at what I'd written. . . . I learned while we were campaigning to speak simply and to tell stories. And that's the way I wrote.

Rosalynn Carter
On writing her autobiography, *First Lady from Plains*. Interview, *The Washington Post*, April 25, 1984.

I'm just someone who has to sit down and think hard about what I want to say. It takes me many drafts. I had to do it in longhand because my computer skills were not up to the task that I'd undertaken.

Hillary Rodham Clinton
On writing her book, *It Takes a Village*; interview, *C-SPAN Booknotes*, March 3, 1996.

There has been so many stories written about me, that I've been thinking of writing one myself in parallel columns, with the fiction that has been written about the things I've done and the places I've seen in one column and the facts in the other.

> **Lou Henry Hoover**
> Comments to the Women's National Press Club, Washington, D.C., February 15, 1933.

It goes in waves of dejection and elation. When I must cut, I become dejected, but when I think a paragraph, a passage captured the mood, I'm elated.

> **Claudia Lady Bird Johnson**
> Describing her memoir-writing project, quoted, *The New York Times*, September 6, 1970.

I always wanted to be some kind of writer or newspaper reporter. But after college I did other things.

> **Jacqueline Kennedy Onassis**
> Comments at book luncheon, New York, January 13, 1977.

I dictate, or sometimes write in longhand, every article or speech which I make.

> **Eleanor Roosevelt**
> White House press conference, March 22, 1935.

I never used a "ghost" in my writings. I like writing too well for that.

> **Eleanor Roosevelt**
> Statement at a literary reception, New York, March 24, 1937.

Of all the world's workers, those which to my mind take by far the highest rank are the writers of noble books.

> **Ellen Axson Wilson**
> Letter to Woodrow Wilson, February 25, 1885.

Youth

Youth is the best season wherein to acquire knowledge, tis a season when we are freest from care, the mind is then unincumbered & more capable of receiving impressions than in an advanced age—in youth the mind is like a tender twig, which you may bend as you please, but in age like a sturdy oak and hard to move.

Abigail Adams
Letter to Isaac Smith, Jr.,
February 7, 1762.

What is youth! that blushing morn

Whose orient beams announce the day

Ah, may no lurking treacherous thorn

Envenom'd round its guiless prey.

Louisa Adams
An addition to a round of poems
started by John Quincy Adams, 1816.

One of the biggest stereotypes in our country right now is about young people, and it really frustrates me because I know first hand that America's young men and women are the best in the entire world.

Hillary Rodham Clinton
Comments at youth rally sponsored
by Team Harmony, Boston,
Massachusetts, December 9, 1997.

Youth never does like supervision and always feels entirely confident that it can handle any situation that arises.

Eleanor Roosevelt
Radio broadcast, *NBC*,
December 23, 1932.

Appendix:
First Ladies and Wives of the Presidents

———— ❧ ————

George Washington
Martha Dandridge Custis
Term as First Lady—April 30, 1789—March 4, 1797
Born—June 21, 1731
Married—January 6, 1759
Died—May 22, 1802

John Adams
Abigail Smith
Term as First Lady—March 4, 1797—March 4, 1801
Born—November 23, 1744
Married—October 25, 1764
Died—October 28, 1818

Thomas Jefferson
Martha Wayles Skelton
Died before Jefferson became president.
Born—October 30, 1748
Married—January 1, 1772
Died—September 6, 1782

James Madison
Dorothea "Dolley" Payne Todd
Term as First Lady—March 4, 1809—March 4, 1817
Born—May 20, 1768
Married—September 15, 1794
Died—July 12, 1849

James Monroe

Elizabeth Kortright
Term as First Lady—March 4, 1817—March 4, 1825
Born—June 30, 1768
Married—February 16, 1786
Died—September 23, 1830

John Quincy Adams

Louisa Catherine Johnson
Term as First Lady—March 4, 1825—March 4, 1829
Born—February 12, 1775
Married—July 26, 1797
Died—May 15, 1852

Andrew Jackson

Rachel Donelson Robards
Died before Jackson was inaugurated president.
Born—June (?), 1767
Married—August (?), 1791. She had married Lewis Robards in 1785.
She married Jackson believing that her first marriage had been legally
    terminated, but her husband had only been granted the right to sue for
    divorce. After a proper divorce decree was issued, she remarried Jackson on
    January 17, 1794.
Died—December 22, 1828

Martin Van Buren

Hannah Hoes
Died before Van Buren was elected president.
Born—March 8, 1783
Married—February 21, 1807
Died—February 5, 1819

William Henry Harrison

Anna Tuthill Symmes
Term as First Lady—March 4, 1841—April 4, 1841
President Harrison died after 31 days in office. Mrs. Harrison, too ill to travel,
    missed the inauguration, and never entered the White House.
Born—July 25, 1775
Married—November 25, 1795
Died—February 25, 1864

John Tyler

Letitia Christian
Term as First Lady—April 6, 1841—September 10, 1842
Born—November 12, 1790
Married—March 29, 1813
Died—September 10, 1842

Julia Gardiner
Term as First Lady—June 26, 1844—March 4, 1845
Born—May 4, 1820
Married—June 26, 1844
Died—July 10, 1889

James K. Polk

Sarah Childress
Term as First Lady—March 4, 1845—March 4, 1849
Born—September 4, 1803
Married—January 1, 1824
Died—August 4, 1891

Zachary Taylor

Margaret Mackall Smith
Term as First Lady—March 5, 1849—July 9, 1850
Since March 4 fell on a Sunday, Taylor was inaugurated president on Monday,
    March 5, 1849. Taylor died in the White House on July 9, 1850.
Born—September 21, 1788
Married—June 21, 1810
Died—August 18, 1852

Millard Fillmore

Abigail Powers
Term as First Lady—July 10, 1850—March 30, 1853
Born—March 13, 1798
Married—February 5, 1826
Died—March 30, 1853

Franklin Pierce

Jane Means Appleton
Term as First Lady—March 4, 1853—March 4, 1857
Born—March 12, 1806
Married—November 19, 1834
Died—December 2, 1863

James Buchanan

Buchanan was a bachelor. His niece Harriet Lane acted as hostess at the White
House during her uncle's term as president, March 4, 1857 to March 4, 1861.

Abraham Lincoln

Mary Ann Todd
Term as First Lady—March 4, 1861—April 15, 1865
President Lincoln was shot by an assassin on April 14, 1865; he died April 15, 1865.
Born—December 13, 1818
Married—November 4, 1842
Died—July 16, 1882

Andrew Johnson

Eliza McCardle
Term as First Lady—April 15, 1865—March 4, 1869
Born—October 4, 1810
Married—May 17, 1827
Died—January 15, 1876

Ulysses S. Grant

Julia Boggs Dent
Term as First Lady—March 4, 1869—March 4, 1877
Born—January 26, 1826
Married—August 22, 1848
Died—December 14, 1902

Rutherford B. Hayes

Lucy Ware Webb
Term as First Lady—March 4, 1877—March 4, 1881
Born—August 28, 1831
Married—December 30, 1852
Died—June 25, 1889

James A. Garfield

Lucretia Rudolph
Term as First Lady—March 4, 1881—September 19, 1881
President Garfield was shot by an assassin July 2, 1881; he died September 19, 1881.
Born—April 19, 1832
Married—November 11, 1858
Died—March 14, 1918

Chester A. Arthur

Ellen Lewis Herndon
Mrs. Arthur died before her husband became president. Arthur's sister Mary
Arthur McElroy assumed the role as White House hostess.
Born—August 30, 1837
Married—October 25, 1859
Died—January 10, 1880

Grover Cleveland

Frances Folsom
Term as First Lady—June 2, 1886—March 4, 1889
March 4, 1893—March 4, 1897
Grover Cleveland was the only man to serve two nonconsecutive terms as
president.
Born—July 21, 1864
Married—June 2, 1886
Died—October 29, 1947

Benjamin Harrison

Caroline Lavinia Scott
Term as First Lady—March 4, 1889—October 25, 1892
Born—October 1, 1832
Married—October 20, 1853
Died—October 25, 1892

William McKinley

Ida Saxton
Term as First Lady—March 4, 1897—September 14, 1901
President McKinley was shot by an assassin
September 6, 1901; he died September 14, 1901.
Born—June 8, 1847
Married—January 25, 1871
Died—May 26, 1907

Theodore Roosevelt

Edith Kermit Carow
Term as First Lady—September 14, 1901—March 4, 1909
Born—August 6, 1861
Married—December 2, 1886
Died—September 30, 1948

William Howard Taft
Helen Herron
Term as First Lady—March 4, 1909—March 4, 1913
Born—June 2, 1861
Married—June 19, 1886
Died—May 22, 1943

Woodrow Wilson
Ellen Louise Axson
Term as First Lady—March 4, 1913—August 6, 1914
Born—May 15, 1860
Married—June 24, 1885
Died—August 6, 1914

Edith Bolling Galt
Term as First Lady—December 18, 1915—March 4, 1921
Born—October 15, 1872
Married—December 18, 1915
Died—December 28, 1961

Warren G. Harding
Florence Kling Dewolfe
Term as First Lady—March 4, 1921—August 2, 1923
President Harding died August 2, 1923.
Born—August 15, 1860
Married—July 8, 1891
Died—November 21, 1924

Calvin Coolidge
Grace Anna Goodhue
Term as First Lady—August 3, 1923—March 4, 1929
Born—January 3, 1879
Married—October 4, 1905
Died—July 8, 1957

Herbert Hoover
Lou Henry
Term as First Lady—March 4, 1929—March 4, 1933
Born—March 29, 1874
Married—February 10, 1899
Died—January 7, 1944

Franklin D. Roosevelt

Anna Eleanor Roosevelt
Term as First Lady—March 4, 1933—April 12, 1945
President Franklin D. Roosevelt died on April 12, 1945.
Born—October 11, 1884
Married—March 17, 1905
Died—November 7, 1962

Harry S. Truman

Elizabeth "Bess" Virginia Wallace
Term as First Lady—April 12, 1945—January 20, 1953
Born—February 13, 1885
Married—June 28, 1919
Died—October 18, 1982

Dwight D. Eisenhower

Marie "Mamie" Geneva Doud
Term as First Lady—January 20, 1953—January 20, 1961
Born—November 14, 1896
Married—July 1, 1916
Died—November 1, 1979

John F. Kennedy

Jacqueline Lee Bouvier
Term as First Lady—January 20, 1961—November 22, 1963
President Kennedy was assassinated on November 22, 1963.
Born—July 28, 1929
Married—September 12, 1953 to John F. Kennedy
Married—October 20, 1968 to Aristotle Onassis
Died—May 19, 1994

Lyndon B. Johnson

Claudia Alta "Lady Bird" Taylor
Term as First Lady—November 22, 1963—January 20, 1969
Born—December 22, 1912
Married—November 17, 1934

Richard M. Nixon

Thelma Catherine Patricia "Pat" Ryan
Term as First Lady—January 20, 1969—August 9, 1974
President Nixon resigned from office on August 9, 1974.
Born—March 16, 1912
Married—June 21, 1940
Died—June 22, 1993

Gerald R. Ford
Elizabeth "Betty" Anne Bloomer
Term as First Lady—August 9, 1974—January 20, 1977
Born—April 8, 1918
Married—October 15, 1948

James Earl "Jimmy" Carter
Rosalynn Smith
Term as First Lady—January 20, 1977—January 20, 1981
Born—August 18, 1927
Married—July 7, 1946

Ronald Reagan
Nancy Davis
Term as First Lady—January 20, 1981—January 20, 1989
Born—July 6, 1923 (This is the official birth date. Mrs. Reagan's high school
    records, however, list her date of birth as July 6, 1921.)
Married—March 4, 1952

George Bush
Barbara Pierce
Term as First Lady—January 20, 1989—January 20, 1993
Born—June 8, 1925
Married—January 5, 1945

William Jefferson "Bill" Clinton
Hillary Rodham
Term as First Lady—January 20, 1993—
Born—October 26, 1947
Married—October 11, 1975

Bibliography

General

Anthony, Carl Sferrazza. *First Ladies, Volume I—The Saga of the Presidents' Wives and Their Power 1789–1961*. New York: Quill, William Morrow, 1990.

Anthony, Carl Sferrazza. *First Ladies, Volume II—The Saga of the Presidents' Wives and Their Power 1961–1990*. New York: Quill, William Morrow, 1990.

Boller, Paul F., Jr. *Presidential Wives*, New York: Oxford University Press, 1988.

Caroli, Betty Boyd. *First Ladies*, New York: Oxford University Press, 1995.

DeGregorio, William A. *The Complete Book of U.S. Presidents*, New York: Barricade Books, 1993.

Furman, Bess. *White House Profile*, Indianapolis: The Bobbs-Merrill Company, Inc., 1951.

Gould, Lewis L., ed. *American First Ladies: Their Life and Their Legacy*, New York: Garland Publishing, Inc., 1996.

Gutin, Myra G. *The President's Partner—The First Lady in the Twentieth Century*, Westport, Conn.: Greenwood Press, 1989.

Heckler-Feltz, Cheryl. *Heart and Soul of the Nation: How the Spirituality of Our First Ladies Changed America*, New York: Doubleday, 1997.

Holloway, Laura C. *The Ladies of the White House: or In the Home of the Presidents*, Philadelphia: A. Gorton & Co., 1882. (Reprinted in 1976 by AMS Press, Inc., New York.)

Klapthor, Margaret Brown. *The First Ladies*, Washington, D.C.: The White House Historical Association, 1994.

Means, Marianne. *The Woman in the White House*, New York: Random House, 1963.

Mennigerode, Meade. *Some American Ladies*, New York: G. P. Putnam's Sons, 1916.

Montgomery, Ruth. *Hail to the Chiefs*, New York: Coward-McCann, Inc., 1970.

Seale, William. *The President's House; A History, Volumes 1 & 2*, Washington, D.C.: White House Historical Association, 1986.

Smith, Nancy Kegan and Ryan, Mary C., eds. *Modern First Ladies: Their Documentary Legacy*, Washington, D.C.: National Archives and Records Administration, 1989.

Thomas, Helen. *Dateline: White House*, New York: Macmillan Publishing Co., Inc., 1975.

Troy, Gil. *Affairs of State*, New York: Free Press, 1997.

Truman, Margaret. *First Ladies*, New York: Random House, 1995.

West, J.B., with Kotz, Mary Lynn. *Upstairs at the White House: My Life With the First Ladies*, New York: Coward, McCann & Geoghegan, Inc., 1973.

Whitton, Mary Ormsbee. *First First Ladies 1789–1865*, Freeport, New York: Books for Libraries Press, 1969.

Abigail Adams

Adams, Charles F., ed. *Correspondence between John Adams and Mercy Warren*, New York: Arno Press, 1972.

Butterfield, L. H.; Friedlaender, Marc; and Kline, Mary-Jo, eds. *The Book of Abigail and John—Selected Letters of the Adams Family 1762–1784*, Cambridge Mass.: Harvard University Press, 1975.

Cappon, Lester J., ed. *The Adams-Jefferson Letters*, Chapel Hill, N.C.: The University of North Carolina Press, 1959.

Ferling, John. *John Adams—A Life*, Knoxville, Tenn.: The University of Tennessee Press, 1992.

Gelles, Edith B. *Portia: The World of Abigail Adams*, Bloomington, Ind.: Indiana University Press, 1992.

Levin, Phyllis Lee. *Abigail Adams*, New York: St. Martin's Press, 1987.

Mitchell, Stewart, ed. *New Letters of Abigail Adams 1788–1801*, Boston: Houghton Mifflin Company, 1947.

Nagel, Paul G. *Adams Women*, New York: Oxford University Press, 1987.

Smith, Page. *John Adams, Volume I 1735–1784*, Garden City, New York: Doubleday, 1962.

Smith, Page. *John Adams, Volume II 1784–1826*, Garden City, New York: Doubleday, 1962.

Louisa Adams

Bobbé, Dorothie. *Mr. & Mrs. John Quincy Adams*, New York: Minton, Balch & Company, 1930.

Hecht, Marie B. *John Quincy Adams*, Newtown, Conn.: American Political Biography Press, 1995.

Nagel, Paul G. *Adams Women*, New York: Oxford University Press, 1987.

Richards, Leonard L. *The Life and Times of Congressman John Quincy Adams*, New York: Oxford University Press, 1986.

Shepherd, Jack. *Cannibals of the Heart: A Personal Biography of Louisa Catherine and John Quincy Adams*, New York: McGraw-Hill Book Company, 1980.

Barbara Bush

Bush, Barbara. *Barbara Bush: A Memoir*, New York: Charles Scribner's Sons, 1994.

Bush, George, with Gold, Victor. *Looking Forward: An Autobiography*, New York: Doubleday, 1987.

Kilian, Pamela. *Barbara Bush: A Biography*, New York: St. Martin's Press, 1992.

Parmet, Herbert S. *George Bush: The Life of a Lone Star Yankee*, New York: A Lisa Drew book, Scribner, 1997.

Radcliffe, Donnie. *Simply Barbara Bush*, New York: Warner Books, Inc., 1989.

Rosalynn Carter

Carter, Jimmy and Rosalynn. *Everything to Gain*, New York: Random House, 1987.

Carter, Rosalynn. *First Lady from Plains*, Boston: Houghton Mifflin Company, 1984.

Carter, Rosalynn. *Helping Yourself Help Others*, New York: Times Books, 1994.

Norton, Howard. *Rosalynn: A Portrait*, Plainfield, New Jersey: Logos International, 1977.

Frances Cleveland

Goodrich, Frederick E. *The Life and Public Service of Grover Cleveland*, Augusta, Maine: E. C. Allen & Company, 1888.

Lynch, Denis Tilden. *Grover Cleveland—A Man Four-Square*, New York: Horace Liveright, Inc., 1932.

Hillary Rodham Clinton

Brock, David. *The Seduction of Hillary Rodham*, New York: The Free Press, 1996.

Clinton, Hillary Rodham. *It Takes a Village: And Other Lessons Children Teach Us*, New York: Simon & Schuster, 1996.

King, Norman. *The Woman in the White House: The Remarkable Hillary Rodham Clinton*, New York: Birch Lane Press Book,1996.

Maraniss, David. *First in His Class: A Biography of Bill Clinton*, Simon & Schuster, 1995.

Radcliffe, Donnie. *Hillary Rodham Clinton: A First Lady for Our Time*, Warner Books, Inc., 1993.

Grace Coolidge

Ross, Ishbel. *Grace Coolidge and Her Era*, New York: Dodd, Mead & Company, 1962.

Wikander, Lawrence E. and Ferrell, Robert H., eds. *Grace Coolidge: An Autobiography*, Worland, Wyoming: High Plains Publishing Company, Inc., 1992.

Mamie Eisenhower

Ambrose, Stephen E. *Eisenhower: The President*, New York: Simon and Schuster, 1984.

David, Lester and David, Irene. *Ike and Mamie: The Story of The General and His Lady*, New York: G. P. Putnam's Sons,1981.

Eisenhower, Susan. *Mrs. Ike: Memories and Reflections on the Life of Mamie Eisenhower*, New York: Farrar, Straus and Giroux, 1996.

Hatch, Alden. *Red Carpet for Mamie*, New York: Henry Holt and Company, 1954.

Abigail Fillmore

Rayback, Robert J. *Millard Fillmore: Biography of a President*, Newtown, Connecticut: American Political Biography Press, 1992.

Betty Ford

Ford, Betty, with Chase, Chris. *The Times of My Life*, New York: Harper & Row, Publishers, Inc., 1978.

Ford, Betty, with Chase, Chris. *Betty, A Glad Awakening*, New York: Doubleday & Company, Inc., 1987.

Ford, Gerald R. *A Time To Heal*, New York: Harper & Row, Publishers, Inc., 1979.

Lucretia Garfield

Booraem, Hendrik V. *The Road to Respectability: James A. Garfield and His World, 1844–1852*, Cranbury, New Jersey: Associated University Presses, Inc., 1988.

Leech, Margaret, and Brown, Harry J. *The Garfield Orbit*, New York: Harper & Row, Publishers, 1978.

Peskin, Allan. *Garfield*, Kent, Ohio: The Kent State University Press, 1978.

Julia Dent Grant

McFeely, William S. *Grant: A Biography*, New York: W. W. Norton & Company, 1982.

Ross, Ishbel. *The General's Wife: The Life of Mrs. Ulysses S. Grant*, New York: Dodd, Mead & Company, 1959.

Simon, John Y., ed. *The Personal Memoirs of Julia Dent Grant* (copyright 1975 by the Ulysses S. Grant Association), New York: G. P. Putnam's Sons, 1975.

Florence Harding

Anthony, Carl Sferrazza. *Florence Harding: The First lady, the Jazz Age, and the Death of America's Most Scandalous President*, New York: William Morrow and Company, Inc., 1998.

Downes, Randolph C. *The Rise of Warren Gamaliel Harding 1865–1920*, Columbus, Ohio: Ohio State University Press, 1970.

Russell, Francis. *The Shadow of Blooming Grove: Warren G. Harding in His Times*, New York: McGraw-Hill Book Company, 1968.

Sinclair, Andrew. *The Available Man: Warren Gamaliel Harding*, New York: The Macmillan Company, 1965.

Lucy Webb Hayes

Geer, Emily Apt. *First Lady: The Life of Lucy Webb Hayes*, Kent, Ohio: The Kent State University Press, 1984.

Hoogenboom, Ari. *Rutherford B.Hayes: Warrior & President*, Lawrence, Kansas: University Press of Kansas, 1995.

Lou Henry Hoover

Mayer, Dale C., ed. *Lou Henry Hoover: Essays on a Busy Life*, Worland, Wyoming: High Plains Publishing Company, Inc., 1994.

Pryor, Helen B. *Lou Henry Hoover—Gallant First Lady*, New York: Dodd, Mead & Company, 1969.

Rachel Jackson

Buell, Augustus C. *History of Andrew Jackson, Volume II*, New York: Charles Scribner's Sons, 1904.

James, Marquis. *The Life of Andrew Jackson*, Indianapolis, Ind.: The Bobbs-Merrill Company, 1938.

Claudia Lady Bird Johnson

Gould, Lewis L. *Lady Bird Johnson and the Environment*, Lawrence, Kansas: University Press of Kansas, 1988.

Johnson, Lady Bird. *A White House Diary*, New York: Holt, Rinehart and Winston, 1970.

Montgomery, Ruth. *Mrs. LBJ*, New York: Holt, Rinehart and Winson, 1964.

Eliza Johnson

Thomas, Lately. *The First President Johnson*, New York: William Morrow & Company, Inc., 1968.

Trefousse, Hans L. *Andrew Johnson: A Biography*, New York: W. W. Norton & Company, 1989.

Jacqueline Kennedy (See Onassis)

Andersen, Christopher. *Jack and Jackie*, New York: William Morrow and Company, Inc., 1996.

Collier, Peter and Horowitz, David. *The Kennedys: An American Drama*, New York: Summit Books, Simon & Schuster, Inc., 1984.

Leamer, Laurence. *The Kennedy Women*, New York: Villard Books, 1994.

Reeves, Richard. *President Kennedy*, New York: Simon & Schuster, 1993.

Schlesinger, Jr., Arthur M. *A Thousand Days: John F. Kennedy in the White House*, Boston: Houghton Mifflin Company, 1965.

Sorenson, Theodore C. *Kennedy*, New York: Harper & Row, Publishers, 1965.

Thayer, Mary Van Rensselaer. *Jacqueline Kennedy: The White House Years*, Boston: Little Brown and Company, 1971.

Mary Todd Lincoln

Baker, Jean H. *Mary Todd Lincoln: A Biography*, New York: W. W. Norton & Company, 1989.

Helm, Katherine. *Mary, Wife of Lincoln*, New York: Harper & Brothers Publishers, 1928.

Neely, Jr. Mark E., and McMurtry, R. Gerald. *The Insanity File: The Case of Mary Todd Lincoln*, Carbondale and Edwardsville, Ill.: Southern Illinois University Press, 1986.

Randall, Ruth Palmer. *Mary Lincoln: Biography of a Marriage*, Boston: Little, Brown and Company, 1953.

Sandburg, Carl; Angle, Paul M. *Mary Lincoln: Wife and Widow*, New York: Harcourt, Brace and Company, Inc., 1932.

Turner, Justin G. and Turner, Linda Levitt. *Mary Todd Lincoln: Her Life and Letters*, New York: Alfred A. Knopf, Inc., 1972.

Dolley Madison

Anthony, Katharine. *Dolly Madison: Her Life and Times*, Garden City, N.Y.: Doubleday & Company, Inc., 1949.

Clark, Allen C. *Life and Letters of Dolly Madison*, Washington, D.C.: W. F. Roberts Company, 1914.

Cutts, Lucia Beverly, ed. *Memoirs and Letters of Dolly Madison*, Boston: Houghton, Mifflin and Company, 1886.

Dean, Elizabeth Lippincott. *Dolly Madison: The Nation's Hostess*, Boston: Lothrop, Lee & Shepard Co., 1928.

Hunt-Jones, Conover. *Dolley and the "Great Little Madison,"* Washington, D.C.: American Institute of Architects Foundation, Inc., 1977.

Ketcham, Ralph. *James Madison: A Biography*, Charlottesville, Virginia: University Press of Virginia, 1990.

Moore, Virginia. *The Madisons: A Biography*, New York: McGraw-Hill Book Company, 1979.

Ida Saxton McKinley

Leech, Margaret. *In the Days of McKinley*, New York: Harper & Brothers, 1959.

Morgan, H. Wayne. *William McKinley and His America*, Syracuse, N.Y.: Syracuse University Press, 1963.

Patricia "Pat" Nixon

Eisenhower, Julie Nixon. *Pat Nixon: The Untold Story*, New York: Simon and Schuster, Inc., 1986.

David, Lester. *The Lonely Lady of San Clemente: The Story of Pat Nixon*, New York: Thomas Y. Crowell, Publishers, 1978.

Nixon, Richard. *RN: The Memoirs of Richard Nixon*, New York: Grosset & Dunlap, 1978.

Jacqueline Kennedy Onassis (See Kennedy)

Andersen, Christopher. *Jackie After Jack*, New York: William Morrow and Company, Inc., 1998.

Birmingham, Stephen. *Jacqueline Bouvier Kennedy Onassis*, New York: Grosset & Dunlap, 1978.

David, Lester. *Jacqueline Kennedy Onassis: A Portrait of Her Private Years*, New York: A Birch Lane Press Book, Carol Publishing Group, 1994.

Heymann, C. David. *A Woman Named Jackie*, New York: A Lyle Stuart Book, Carol Communications, 1989.

Kelley, Kitty. *Jackie Oh!* Secaucus, New Jersey: Lyle Stuart, 1978.

Jane Pierce

Boas, Norman F. *Jane M. Pierce: The Pierce-Aiken Papers*, Stonington, Conn.: Seaport Autographs, 1983.

Nichols, Roy Franklin. *Franklin Pierce: Young Hickory of the Granite Hills*, Newtown, Conn.: American Political Biography Press, 1993.

Sarah Childress Polk

Bumgarner, John Reed. *Sarah Childress Polk: A Biography of the Remarkable First Lady*, Jefferson, N.C.: McFarland & Company, Inc., Publishers, 1997.

Nelson, Anson and Nelson, Fanny. *Memorials of Sarah Childress Polk*, New York: Anson D. F. Randolph & Company, 1892.(Reprinted by American Political Biography Press, Newtown, Conn., 1994.)

Nancy Reagan

Kelley, Kitty. *Nancy Reagan: The Unauthorized Biography*, New York: Simon & Schuster, Inc., 1991.

Leamer, Laurence. *Make-Believe: The Story of Nancy and Ronald Reagan*, New York: Harper & Row, Publishers, 1983.

Reagan, Nancy, with Libby, Bill. *Nancy*, New York: William Morrow and Company, 1980.

Reagan, Nancy, with Novak, William. *My Turn: The Memoirs of Nancy Reagan*, New York: Random House, 1989.

Wallace, Chris. *First Lady: A Portrait of Nancy Reagan*, New York: St. Martin's Press, 1986.

Edith Kermit Roosevelt

Hagedorn, Hermann, *The Roosevelt Family of Sagamore Hill*, New York: The Macmillan Company, 1954.

Morris, Sylvia Jukes. *Edith Kermit Roosevelt: Portrait of a First Lady*, New York: Coward, McCann & Geoghegan, Inc., 1980.

Roosevelt, Edith Kermit, et al. *Cleared for Strange Ports*, New York: Charles Scribner's Sons, 1927.

Eleanor Roosevelt

Black, Allida M. *Casting Her Own Shadow: Eleanor Roosevelt and the Shaping of Postwar Liberalism*, New York: Columbia University Press, 1996.

Cook, Blanche Wiesen. *Eleanor Roosevelt Vol. I: 1884–1933*, New York: Viking Penguin, Penguin Books USA, Inc., 1992.

Faber, Doris. *The Life of Lorena Hickok: L E.R.'s Friend*, New York: William Morrow & Company, Inc., 1980.

Lash, Joseph P. *Eleanor and Franklin*, New York: W. W. Norton & Company, Inc., 1971.

Lash, Joseph P. *Love, Eleanor: Eleanor Roosevelt and Her Friends*, New York: Doubleday & Company, Inc., 1982.

Lash, Joseph P. *Eleanor: The Years Alone*, New York: W. W. Norton & Company, 1972.

Lash, Joseph P. *A World of Love: Eleanor Roosevelt and Her Friends, 1943–1962*, New York: Doubleday & Company 1984.

Roosevelt, Eleanor. *This Is My Story*, New York: Harper & Brothers, Publishers, 1937.

Roosevelt, Eleanor. *This I Remember*, New York: Harper & Brothers, 1949.

Roosevelt, Eleanor. *Tomorrow Is Now*, New York: Harper & Row, Publishers, 1963.

Roosevelt, Eleanor. *The Autobiography of Eleanor Roosevelt*, New York: Da Capo Press Inc., 1992.

Roosevelt, Elliott and Brough, James. *Mother R: Eleanor Roosevelt's Untold Story*, New York: G. P. Putnam's Sons, 1977.

Helen Taft

Pringle, Henry F. *The Life and Times of William Howard Taft, Volumes 1 and 2*, New York: Holt, Rinehart and Winston, Inc., 1939. (Reprinted in 1964 by Archon Books, Hamden, Conn.)

Taft, Helen Herron. *Recollections of Full Years*, New York: Dodd, Mead & Company, 1914.

Bess Truman

Ferrell, Robert H., editor. *Dear Bess: The Letters from Harry to Bess Truman 1910–1959*, New York: W. W. Norton & Company, 1983.

McCullough, David. *Truman*, New York: Simon & Schuster, 1992.

St. Johns, Adela Rogers. *Some Are Born Great*, New York: Doubleday & Company, 1974.

Truman, Margaret. *Souvenir: Margaret Truman's Own Story*, New York: McGraw-Hill Book Company, Inc., 1956.

Truman, Margaret. *Bess W. Truman*, New York: Macmillan Publishing Company, 1986.

Underhill, Robert. *The Truman Persuasions*, Ames, Iowa: The Iowa State University Press, 1981.

Julia Gardiner Tyler

Chitwood, Oliver Perry. *John Tyler: Champion of the Old South*, Newtown, Conn.: American Political Biography Press, 1990.

Seager, Robert II. *And Tyler too: A Biography of John & Julia Gardiner Tyler*, New York: McGraw-Hill Book Company, Inc., 1963.

Martha Washington

Caroll, John Alexander and Ashworth, Mary Wells (completing the biography by Douglas Southall Freeman). *George Washington, Volume Seven*, New York: Charles Scribner's Sons, 1957.

Fields, Joseph E. *"Worthy Partner": The Papers of Martha Washington*, Westport, Conn.: Greenwood Press, 1994.

Freeman, Douglas Southall. *George Washington, Volume Six*, New York: Charles Scribner's Sons, 1954.

Wharton, Anne Hollingsworth. *Martha Washington*, New York: Charles Scribner's Sons, 1897.

Edith Wilson

Hatch, Alden. *Edith Bolling Wilson: First Lady Extraordinary*, New York: Dodd, Mead & Company, 1962.

Shachtman, Tom. *Edith & Woodrow*, New York: G. P. Putnam's Sons, 1981.

Tribble, Edwin, ed. *A President in Love*, Boston: Houghton Mifflin Company, 1981.

Wilson, Edith Bolling. *My Memoir*, Indianapolis: The Bobbs-Merrill Company, 1939.

Ellen Axson Wilson

Heckscher, August. *Woodrow Wilson: A Biography*, New York: Charles Scribner's Sons, 1991.

McAdoo, Eleanor Wilson. *The Priceless Gift—The Love Letters of Woodrow Wilson and Ellen Axson Wilson*, New York: McGraw-Hill Book Company, Inc., 1962.

Saunders, Frances Wright. *Ellen Axson Wilson: First Lady Between Two Worlds*, Chapel Hill, N.C: The University of North Carolina Press, 1985.

Newspapers/News Organizations

Associated Press
Atlanta Constitution
Atlanta Journal
Baltimore Sun
Boston Globe
Boston Herald
Chicago Daily News
Cincinnati Graphic News
Group W. News
Houston Post
International Herald Tribune (Paris)
Kaybam International
Los Angeles Times
New York Herald Tribune
New York Journal
New York Post
New York Times
Ontario Windsor Star
Philadelphia Inquirer
Philadelphia Press
PM
Reuters News Agency
Richmond Inquirer
San Antonio Express
Toledo Times
Trenton Evening Times
St. Louis Globe-Democrat
St. Louis Post-Dispatch
United Press International
USA Today
Washington Post
Washington Star
Washington Times
Washington Times-Herald

Periodicals

American Magazine
Body Mind Spirit
Current History
Glamour
Good Housekeeping
House Beautiful
Harvard Educational Review
Ladies' Home Journal
Land Policy Review
Life
Literary Digest
Look
McCall's
Modern Maturity
Ms. Magazine
The Nation
The New Republic
Newsday's Magazine for Long Island
Newsweek
New York Times Book Review
New York Times Magazine
The New Yorker
Parade Magazine
People
Reader's Digest
Redbook
Time
Today's Health
True Confessions
U.S. News & World Report
Vanity Fair
Woman's Day
Woman's Home Companion

Acknowledgments

Researching and compiling quotes for this book was a great journey which, in a sense, took me into the private and public life of our First Ladies, the wives of the presidents of the United States.

Researching can often become a drudgery, but my work was lightened and made enjoyable by the supply and cooperation of many people.

The various presidential libraries and museums, along with the National Archives and Library of Congress, offered treasure troves of information and quotable material from our First Ladies.

I wish to give thanks for the special help given to me by—

Leesa Tobin, Archivist, Gerald R. Ford Library, Ann Arbor, Michigan;
Dale C. Mayer, ACA, Archivist, Herbert Hoover Library, West Branch, Iowa;
Linda M. Seelke, Archivist, Lyndon Baines Johnson Library, Austin, Texas;
James Wagner, Public Relations Staff, and June Payne, Reference Staff, John Fitzgerald Kennedy Library, Boston, Massachusetts;
Elizabeth Safly, Librarian, Harry S. Truman Library, Independence, Missouri;
Cyndy Bittinger, Executive Director, The Calvin Coolidge Memorial Foundation, Inc., Plymouth Rock, Vermont.

I am grateful to The Ulysses S. Grant Association for permission to reprint certain passages from the book, "The Personal Memoirs of Julia Dent Grant," 1975, edited by John Y. Simon.

I have strived to identify sources of the quotations, whether they were obtained from correspondence, memoirs, books, magazines or newspapers.

Particular thanks must go to the staff of the Virginia Beach Public Library who patiently and enthusiastically assisted me in bringing this work to fruition.

Index